Thomas Middleton

A MAD WORLD MY MASTERS

Edited by Sean Foley and Phil Porter

OBERON BOOKS
LONDON

WWW.OBERONBOOKS.COM

First published in 2013 by Oberon Books Ltd
521 Caledonian Road, London N7 9RH
Tel: +44 (0) 20 7607 3637 / Fax: +44 (0) 20 7607 3629
e-mail: info@oberonbooks.com
www.oberonbooks.com

A catalogue record for this book is available from the British
Library.

PB ISBN: 978-1-78319-019-5
E ISBN: 978-1-78319-518-3

Cover image by © Rachel Rebibo / Arcangel Images

Printed, bound and converted
by CPI Group (UK) Ltd, Croydon, CR0 4YY.

Visit www.oberonbooks.com to read more about all our books
and to buy them. You will also find features, author interviews and
news of any author events, and you can sign up for e-newsletters
so that you're always first to hear about our new releases.

ABOUT THE ROYAL SHAKESPEARE COMPANY

The Shakespeare Memorial Theatre opened in Stratford-upon-Avon in 1879. Since then the plays of Shakespeare have been performed here, alongside the work of his contemporaries and of modern playwrights. In 1960 the Royal Shakespeare Company was formed, gaining its Royal Charter in 1961.

The founding Artistic Director, Peter Hall, created an ensemble theatre company of young actors and writers. The Company was led by Hall, Peter Brook and Michel Saint-Denis. The founding principles were threefold: the Company would embrace the freedom and power of Shakespeare's work, train and develop young actors and directors and, crucially, experiment in new ways of making theatre. There was a new spirit amongst this post-war generation and they intended to open up Shakespeare's plays as never before.

The impact of Peter Hall's vision cannot be underplayed. In 1955 he premiered Samuel Beckett's *Waiting for Godot* in London, and the result was like opening a window during a storm. The tumult of new ideas emerging across Europe in art, theatre and literature came flooding into British theatre. Hall channelled this new excitement into the setting up of the Company in Stratford. Exciting breakthroughs took place in the rehearsal room and the studio day after day. The RSC became known for exhilarating performances of Shakespeare alongside new masterpieces such as *The Homecoming* and *Old Times* by Harold Pinter. It was a combination that thrilled audiences.

Peter Hall's rigour on classical text became legendary, but what is little known is that he applied everything he learned working on Beckett, and later on Harold Pinter, to his work on Shakespeare, and likewise he applied everything he learned from Shakespeare onto modern texts. This close and exacting relationship between writers from different eras became the fuel which powered the creativity of the RSC.

The search for new forms of writing and directing was led by Peter Brook. He pushed writers to experiment. "Just as Picasso set out to capture a larger slice of the truth by painting a face with several eyes and noses, Shakespeare, knowing that man is living his everyday life and at the same time is living intensely in the invisible world of his thoughts and feelings, developed a method through which we can see at one and the same time the look on a man's face and the vibrations of his brain."

In our fifty years of producing new plays, we have sought out some of the most exciting writers of their generation. These have included: Edward Albee, Howard Barker, Edward Bond, Howard Brenton, Marina Carr, Caryl Churchill, Martin Crimp, David Edgar, Helen Edmundson, James Fenton, Georgia Fitch, David Greig, Dennis Kelly, Tarell Alvin McCraney, Martin McDonagh, Frank McGuinness, Rona Munro, Anthony Neilson, Harold Pinter, Phil Porter, Mike Poulton, Mark Ravenhill, Adriano Shaplin, Tom Stoppard, debbie tucker green and Roy Williams.

The Company today is led by Gregory Doran, whose recent appointment represents a long-term commitment to the disciplines and craftsmanship required to put on the plays of Shakespeare. He, along with Executive Director, Catherine Mallyon, and his Deputy Artistic Director, Erica Whyman, will take forward a belief in celebrating both Shakespeare's work and the work of his contemporaries, as well as inviting some of the most exciting theatre-makers of today to work with the Company on new plays.

The RSC Ensemble is generously supported by THE GATSBY CHARITABLE FOUNDATION and THE KOVNER FOUNDATION.

The RSC is grateful for the significant support of its principal funder, Arts Council England, without which our work would not be possible. Around 50 per cent of the RSC's income is self-generated from Box Office sales, sponsorship, donations, enterprise and partnerships with other organisations.

Supported using public funding by
ARTS COUNCIL ENGLAND

NEW WORK AT THE RSC

We are a contemporary theatre company built on classical rigour. We commission playwrights to engage with the muscularity and ambition of the classics. We have recently re-launched the RSC Studio to resource writers, directors and actors to explore and develop new ideas for our stages. We invite writers to spend time with us in our rehearsal rooms, with our actors and practitioners. Alongside developing their own plays for our stages, we invite them to contribute dramaturgically to both our main stage Shakespeare productions and our Young People's Shakespeare.

We believe that our writers help to establish a creative culture within the Company which both inspires new work and creates an ever more urgent sense of enquiry into the classics. The benefits work both ways. With our writers, our actors naturally learn the language of dramaturgical intervention and sharpen their interpretation of roles. Our writers benefit from re-discovering the stagecraft and theatre skills that have been lost over time. They regain the knack of writing roles for leading actors. They become hungry to use classical structures to power up their plays.

Pippa Hill is our Literary Manager and Mark Ravenhill is our Playwright in Residence.

The RSC Literary Department is generously supported by THE DRUE HEINZ TRUST. CROSS is the exclusive pen partner of the RSC in support of New Work.

This production of *A Mad World My Masters* was first performed by the Royal Shakespeare Company in the Swan Theatre, Stratford-upon-Avon, on 6 June 2013. The cast was as follows:

WAITER/SERVANT/A LOCAL	**Joe Bannister**
MRS LITTLEDICK	**Ellie Beaven**
MRS KIDMAN	**Ishia Bennison**
SPONGER	**Ben Deery**
SPUNKY	**Richard Durden**
DICK FOLLYWIT	**Richard Goulding**
PENITENT BROTHEL	**John Hopkins**
SINGER	**Linda John-Pierre**
CARETAKER/ SIR AQUITAINE SQUODGE/ A LOCAL	**Gwilym Lloyd**
OBOE	**Harry McEntire**
WAITER/RENT BOY	**Perry Millward**
MASTER WHOPPING-PROSPECT	**Ciarán Owens**
MASTER MUCHLY-MINTED	**Nicholas Prasad**
SIR BOUNTEOUS PEERSUCKER	**Ian Redford**
ESCORT/PROSTITUTE	**Rose Reynolds**
MR LITTLEDICK	**Steffan Rhodri**
TRULY KIDMAN	**Sarah Ridgeway**
PRIVATE DETECTIVE/ SIR SKUNKNODGER	**David Rubin**
WAITRESS/ PROSTITUTE/SERVANT	**Badria Timimi**
CONSTABLE	**Dwane Walcott**
WAITER/SERVANT/A LOCAL	**Jonny Weldon**

All other parts played by members of the Company.

Directed by	**Sean Foley**
Designed by	**Alice Power**
Lighting Designed by	**James Farncombe**
Music and Sound by	**Ben and Max Ringham**
Choreography by	**Kate Prince**
Fights by	**Alison de Burgh**
Dance Repetiteur	**Polly Bennett**
Company Text and Voice Work by	**Stephen Kemble**
Assistant Director	**Marieke Audsley**
Music Director	**John Woolf**
Casting by	**Hannah Miller** CDG
Literary Manager	**Pippa Hill**
Production Manager	**Peter Griffin**
Costume Supervisor	**Sam Pickering**
Company Manager	**Michael Dembowicz**
Stage Manager	**Pip Horobin**
Deputy Stage Manager	**Jenny Grand**
Assistant Stage Manager	**Christie Gerrard**

MUSICIANS

Trumpet	**Andrew Stone-Fewings**
Trombone	**Kevin Pitt**
Guitar	**Tom Durham**
Bass	**Roger Inniss**
Drum kit	**James Jones**
Keyboards	**John Woolf**

This text may differ slightly from the play as performed.

JOIN US

Join us from £18 a year.

Join today and make a difference

The Royal Shakespeare Company is an ensemble. We perform all year round in our Stratford-upon-Avon home, as well as having regular seasons in London, and touring extensively within the UK and overseas for international residencies.

With a range of options from £18 to £10,000 per year, there are many ways to engage with the RSC.

Choose a level that suits you and enjoy a closer connection with us whilst also supporting our work on stage.

Find us online

Sign up for regular email updates at **www.rsc.org.uk/signup**

Join today

Annual RSC Full Membership costs just £40 (or £18 for Associate Membership) and provides you with regular updates on RSC news, advance information and priority booking.

Support us

A charitable donation from £100 a year can offer you the benefits of membership, whilst also allowing you the opportunity to deepen your relationship with the Company through special events, backstage tours and exclusive ticket booking services.

The options include Shakespeare's Circle (from £100), Patrons' Circle (Silver: £1,000, Gold: £5,000) and Artists' Circle (£10,000).

For more information visit **www.rsc.org.uk/joinus** or call the RSC Membership Office on 01789 403 440.

THE ROYAL SHAKESPEARE COMPANY

Editors' note

Thomas Middleton's *A Mad World My Masters* is one of the most hilariously wicked plays ever written. If new, it might be hailed as the bastard offspring of Richard Sheridan and Joe Orton, but one whose midwife was a nurse from a 1970s sex comedy. As outrageous as anything you might find on Channel 4, yet as hilarious as any classic mainstream comedy, the play manages to be satirical yet celebratory. It reads as a compendium – almost a masterclass – in juggling differing comic styles: it mixes profound wit and slapstick, poetics and vaudevillian jokes, and biting class comedy with filthy innuendo. Yet Middleton's genius still manages to keep us interested in the fantastical story, and the marvellous parade of characters striving to find their way to love and fortune in a recognisably fast-paced London.

We wanted to make sure that nothing got in the way of communicating Middleton's seething delight in exposing how we pretend to be what we're not to get what we want. He shows how lustful, vain, greedy and desperate we are, and how hard we work to cover this with threadbare conventional morality. We wanted to underline the playful way he develops his plots, and how he plays with the idea of theatre itself; because the whole play is a sort of vibrant amoral celebration of entertainment – it knows it's being funny, and invites us to have fun in knowing that it knows. And we wanted to try to make sure everyone could laugh like they must have done in 1608: uproariously, and at ourselves.

So, in editing and adapting, we decided to cut away innuendoes, references, and allusions to things no one has heard of any more. We removed around a fifth of the original play, and re-visited or even re-wrote some passages – while doing our best to impersonate the salty Middleton tang. We have occasionally changed character names where Middleton's joke could be rendered more clearly with modern language. And we have 'translated' from his Jacobean English into our own contemporary idioms in those few passages where we judged that Middleton's intentions and humour would be too buried in inaccessible language.

London is timeless, and 1950s Soho seemed to offer a stylish and recognisable stand-in for London 1608: a post-war world where everyone is worried about sliding morals, the position of women, a changing class system, immigrants, and where on earth to get the next drink. But this is also a time when 'you've never had it so good', and when foreign fashions and food began loosening straight-laced Britain, despite the high-minded protestations of some.

In the end, we adapted and edited *A Mad World My Masters* – and the RSC decided to produce it – because it's a still magnificently alive play. It celebrates and castigates our obsessions with sex and money – how we buy the one, and make love to the other – and does so with such fun and brio that it's, well, *undecent.*

Sean Foley and Phil Porter

Characters

SIR BOUNTEOUS PEERSUCKER,
an old and wealthy knight

DICK FOLLYWIT,
grand-nephew to Sir Bounteous

MISS TRULY KIDMAN,
a prostitute

MR LITTLEDICK,
a jealous husband

MRS LITTLEDICK,
wife to Mr Littledick

MR PENITENT BROTHEL,
in love with Mrs Littledick

(SERGEANT) SPONGER and (PRIVATE) OBOE,
Follywit's cohorts

MRS KIDMAN,
her daughter's pimp

SPUNKY,
Butler to Sir Bounteous

SUCCUBUS,
a she-devil in the likeness of Mrs Littledick

CARETAKER,
of Mr Penitent Brothel's bedsit

MASTER MUCHLY-MINTED and
MASTER WHOPPING-PROSPECT,
suitors to Miss Truly Kidman

SIR ANDREW SKUNKNODGER and
SIR AQUITAINE SQUODGE,
visitors to Sir Bounteous

CONSTABLE

PRIVATE DETECTIVE,
hired by Mr Littledick, a client of Miss Truly
Kidman's

SERVANTS
to Sir Bounteous

WAITERS/WAITRESSES
at The Flamingo Club and The Moka Bar

1.1

The Flamingo Club, 1956, Soho.

The HOUSE BAND strike up… As the characters of the play enter, they acknowledge members of the audience as old friends, or fellow punters…

The Singer belts out…

> SONG: *'BIG LONG SLIDIN' THING'* by Eddie Kirkland and Mamie Thomas

In the applause at the end of the song DICK FOLLYWIT leaps onto the stage and attempts to kiss the singer. His ardour is not reciprocated. A massive FIGHT breaks out, spreading to include everyone…

…and ending with FOLLYWIT and his cohorts being thrown out, drunk, laughing and bloodied, into a rubbish-filled and piss-soaked back alley…

OBOE: What shall I call thee, Master Dick Follywit? The noble spark of bounty, the life-blood of Society!

SPONGER: A very rascal! A midnight surfeiter! The spume of a brothel-house!

FOLLYWIT: Call me your Brains Trust, you sons of whores. When you come drunk out of a tavern, 'tis I must cast your plots into form still; 'tis I must manage the prank if we're to earn a louse; 'tis I must risk my social standing, turn wild-brain and stretch my wits upon the tenters… You have no occupation but sleep, feed and fart.

SPONGER: Ooh, nothing conjures up wit sooner than poverty! Our little Brains Trust!

FOLLYWIT: Hang you, you have bewitched me among you. 'Til I fell to be wicked I was well born. I went all in black, never did blaspheme, never came home drunk. God's eyelid, here's a transformation! My own Uncle wouldn't know me… Now I'm put i'th'mind of a trick, can you keep your countenance, Private Oboe?

OBOE: I shall keep my face straight.

FOLLYWIT: Then, thus… Have I ever told of the possibilities of my hereafter fortunes, and the humour of my uncle, Sir Bounteous Peersucker?

SPONGER: Never! *(Aside.)* Time without number he has us this recounted!

FOLLYWIT: His death makes all possible to me: I shall have all when he has nothing; but now he has all, I shall have nothing. And since he has no will to do me good as long as he lives, by mine own will, I will do my self good before he dies, I will. And now I arrive at the purpose.

OBOE: At last.

FOLLYWIT: You are not ignorant, I'm sure, you true and necessary implements of mischief, first, that my uncle Sir Bounteous is tremendously well-endowed; next, that he keeps a house like a Shoreditch wench's legs, open to all comers; thirdly and lastly, that he stands much upon the glory of his complement, the fecundity of his larder, and the glorious generosity of his fancy dress balls. He's a snoblick of the first – mere Sir's or Ladies impress him not, but he thinks himself never happier then when some stiff Lord or country Countess alights, to make light his dishes. Fancying them his friends he bends backwards like a fool as they chomp on his tenderloin, and ne'er thinks e'en to ask them to sauce his asparagus as they gobble him dry.

SPONGER: Come again?

FOLLYWIT: These ingredients being well mixed together may give my project better encouragement. To be short, and cut off a great deal of dirty way, I'll down to my uncle like a lord.

SPONGER: How, captain?

FOLLYWIT: I shall tell you – Sergeant Sponger! Private Oboe!

OBOE: Sir.

FOLLYWIT: An Italian suit, a thin moustache and a strong perfume will do't. I'll live like a Lord at his expense, and you shall be my servants.

SPONGER: You're mad, sir.

FOLLYWIT: Me, mad?! You desire crowns?

SPONGER AND OBOE: Ay Captain!

FOLLYWIT: Why, then carry yourselves but plausibly and you'll carry away plenty.

OBOE: *(In awe.)* The noble spark of Bounty!

Enter PENITENT BROTHEL.

FOLLYWIT: Mr Penitent Brothel.

BROTHEL: Sweet Master Follywit.

Exeunt all but BROTHEL.

BROTHEL: Here's a mad-brain o'th'first, whose pranks scorn to have precedents, whose only glory is to be prime of the company, to be sure of which he maintains all the rest. He is the carrion and they the kites that gorge upon him.
But why in others do I check wild passions
And retain deadly follies in myself?
I tax his youth of common receiv'd riot,
Time's comic flashes, and the fruits of blood;
And in myself soothe up adulterous motions:
Love to the wife of Mr Littledick,
Over whose hours and pleasures her sick husband,
With a fantastic but deserved jealousy,
Bestows his serious time in watch and ward.
And therefore I'm constrained to use a prostitute,
Whom Mr Littledick
without suspicion innocently admits
To his wife's company, who with tried art
Corrupts and loosens his wife's most constant powers.

Enter TRULY KIDMAN.

TRULY KIDMAN: Mister Brothel.

BROTHEL: See, here she comes; a virtuous, well brought up whore – her mother is her pimp! Miss Truly Kidman. The news, the comfort?

TRULY KIDMAN: Y'are the fortunate man, sir. There wants but opportunity and she's wax of your own fashioning. She had wrought herself into the form of your love before my art set finger to her.

BROTHEL: Did our affections meet? Our thoughts keep time?

TRULY KIDMAN: So it should seem by the music. The only jar is in that grumbling base fiddle, her husband.

BROTHEL: Oh, his waking suspicion!

TRULY KIDMAN: Sigh not, Mr Brothel. Trust the managing of the business with me; 'tis for my credit now to see't well finished.

BROTHEL: Heart, I would give but too much money to be nibbling with that wench!

TRULY KIDMAN: If I do you no good, sir, you shall give me no money, sir.

BROTHEL: O admirable times! An honest whore. Farewell, lady.

Exit PENITENT BROTHEL. TRULY KIDMAN walks on and finds herself outside The Moka Bar. Enter MRS KIDMAN. They sit at a table. TRULY KIDMAN drops her act, revealing herself to be, like her mother, as common as muck…

MRS KIDMAN: How now daughter?

TRULY KIDMAN: Alright, mother? Cuh, what strange impudence governs in man when lust is lord of him. What news?

MRS KIDMAN: A token from thy keeper.

TRULY KIDMAN: Oh, from Sir Bounteous Peersucker. I've never had a pearl necklace before. He's my keeper indeed, but there's plenty more who've poached this piece o'chicken. I been spatchcocked, trussed up, boned and basted more times than he's had hot caudle.

MRS KIDMAN: Hold thee there, girl!

TRULY KIDMAN: Fear not me, mother.

MRS KIDMAN: But I do, when every part of the world shoots up daily into more subtlety.
The shallow ploughman can distinguish now,
'Twixt simple truth and a dissembling brow.
How does't behoove us then that live by sleight,
To have our wits wound up to their stretched height!
Fifteen times thou know'st I've stitched
and peddled thy virgin puss,
To make up a dowry for thy marriage.
The sums I have done upon thy pillows!
But still you'll play the chaste virgin, my girl.
The Italian is not serviced yet, nor the French;
And the British men lurk in the doorway but never come inside.
Remember 'tis nothing but a cunning stunt,
A sincere carriage, a religious eyebrow
To cast a spell over the worldlings' senses.

WAITRESS: Yeah!

MRS KIDMAN: And when thou spiest a fool that truly pities
The false springs of thine eyes,
And honourably dotes upon thy love,
If he be rich set him by for a husband.
Be wisely tempered and learn this my wench:
Who gets th'opinion for a virtuous name
May sin at pleasure and ne'er think of shame.

TRULY KIDMAN: Mother, I am too deep a scholar grown
To learn my first rules now.

MRS KIDMAN: I say no more.

Enter MASTER MUCHLY-MINTED and MASTER WHOPPING-PROSPECT.

MASTER WHOPPING-PROSPECT
AND MASTER MUCHLY-MINTED: Hello!

MRS KIDMAN: Peace, hark, remove thyself. Potential husbands!

TRULY KIDMAN scarpers…

MASTER WHOPPING-PROSPECT : A fair hour, sweet lady.

MRS KIDMAN: *(Posh again.)* Good morrow, gentlemen, Master Muchly-Minted, Master Whopping-Prospect.

MASTER MUCHLY-MINTED: Where's the little sweet lady your daughter gone?

MRS KIDMAN: To read her bible, sir.

MASTER WHOPPING-PROSPECT: So religious?

MRS KIDMAN: 'Tis no new motion, sir, she's at it all hours.

MASTER MUCHLY-MINTED: And her mountains? She is heir, is she not, to some nineteen mountains?

MRS KIDMAN: That she is, sir. And all as high as Saint Paul's.

MASTER WHOPPING-PROSPECT: May we see a sight of her, lady?

MRS KIDMAN: Upon that condition you will promise me, gentlemen, to avoid all profane talk, wanton complements, undecent phrases, and lascivious courtings (which I know my daughter will sooner die then endure), I am contented your suits shall be granted.

MASTER WHOPPING-PROSPECT: Not a bawdy syllable, I protest.

MASTER MUCHLY-MINTED: Syllable was well-placed there, for, indeed, your one syllables are your bawdiest words: prick that down!

1.2

At the Littledick house. MR LITTLEDICK's study.

MR LITTLEDICK: I'll be at charge for watch and ward, I'll watch and ward her I'faith. She may make night work on't! Tomcats and whores stroll most i'th'night. Tis the time for Clap-fallen daughters, night-walking widows, libidinous wives! Her friend may be received nightly! Yes, I'll watch and ward her. And here he is.

Enter a cheap PRIVATE DETECTIVE.

DETECTIVE: At your service, Mister Littledick.

MR LITTLEDICK: Welcome, my friend. I must request your diligence in an employment serious. The truth is, there is a cunning plot laid, but happily discovered, to rob my house, the night uncertain when, but fixed within the circle of this month. Nor does this villainy consist in numbers; some one may, in the form of my familiar friend – I'll not say his name, but 'tis Penitent Brothel – be slipped cunningly into my wife's private chamber.

DETECTIVE: O, abominable!

MR LITTLEDICK: If you be a faithful watchman, show your goodness, and with these beauties shore up your eyelids. *(He gives him money.)* Let me not be purloined. There is a lady's ruby I would not lose, kept by the jealous Italian-type under lock and key: we English men are careless creatures. Well, I have said enough!

DETECTIVE: And I will do enough, sir.

MR LITTLEDICK: Why, well said. Watch me a good turn now.

Exit DETECTIVE.

MR LITTLEDICK: So, so, so.
Rise villainy with the lark, why, 'tis prevented,
Or steal't by with the leather winged Bat,
The night cannot protect it. Peace – her moral tutor.

Enter TRULY KIDMAN dressed as a nun.

MR LITTLEDICK: Oh Sister Kidman, my wife's only company, welcome!

TRULY KIDMAN: Mr Littledick.

MR LITTLEDICK: And how does the virtuous matron, thy mother? A woman of an excellent carriage all her lifetime, in court, city and country.

TRULY KIDMAN: She's always carried it well in those places, sir – *(Aside.)* three bastards from each. *(To MR LITTLEDICK.)* How does your sweet bed-fellow, sir?

MR LITTLEDICK: I left her within, stroking at her lute, prithee give her good counsel.

TRULY KIDMAN: Alas, she needs none, sir.

MR LITTLEDICK: Yet, yet, yet, a little of thy instructions will not come amiss to her.

TRULY KIDMAN: I'll bestow my labour, sir.

MR LITTLEDICK: Do, labour her prithee. I have conveyed away all her wanton pamphlets, 'Venus and Adonis', her *Health and Efficiency* magazine. Oh, two luscious mary-bone pies for a young married wife! Here, here, prithee, take this bible and read to her a little.

TRULY KIDMAN: Revelations, sir?

MR LITTLEDICK: There's a chapter of hell, 'tis good to read, terrify her, terrify her; read to her the horrible punishments for itching wantonness, the pains alotted for adultery; tell her her thoughts, her very dreams are answerable.

Enter MRS LITTLEDICK.

TRULY KIDMAN: I shall lay bare the life of a filthy prostitute and show how loathsome 'tis.

He goes in to the next room…

MRS LITTLEDICK: Fain would I meet Mr Brothel. The more I look on him the more I thirst for it.

TRULY KIDMAN: Push, I know it.

In the other room…

MR LITTLEDICK: This is the course I take; I'll teach the
  married man
  A new selected strain, I admit none
  But this pure virgin to her company,
  And so I'll keep her to her stint,
  I'll put her to her pension,
  I'll give her her allowance.
  Ha, ha, ha, nay, I'll put her hard to't.

Back in the study…

MRS LITTLEDICK: Tell me, Truly, how will I meet the
  gentleman? By what means shall we come together?

TRULY KIDMAN: Shall I have a hearing, listen…

MR LITTLEDICK: *(Listening through the wall.)*
  How earnestly she labours her. She will prevail, I hope.

TRULY KIDMAN: When husbands in their rank'st suspitions
  dwell,
  Then 'tis our best art to dissemble well.
  Put but these notes in use that I'll direct you,
  He'll curse himself that e'er he did suspect you.
  Perhaps he will solicit you, as in trial,
  To visit such and such; still give denial.
  Let no persuasions sway you,
  Seem in his sight to endure the sight of no man.
  Neglect to entertain; if he bring in
  Strangers, keep you your chamber, be not seen;
  If he chance steal upon you, let him find
  Some book lying open 'gainst an unchaste mind,

MR LITTLEDICK: *(Still listening.)* She's round with her i'faith.

TRULY KIDMAN: Though for your own pleasure
  You read some stirring pamphlet, and convey it
  Under your skirt, the fittest place to stick it.

MRS LITTLEDICK exclaims…

TRULY KIDMAN: This is the course, my wench, to enjoy thy
wishes.

Manage these principles but with Art and life;

And in front of all men thou'rt an honest wife.

MR LITTLEDICK: *(Still listening.)* She puts it home i'faith, even
to the quick.

I must requite this maid – faith, I'm forgetful.

MRS LITTLEDICK: Here, lady, convey my heart unto him in
this jewel.

Against you see me next you shall perceive

I have profited. In the meantime tell Mr Brothel

I am a prisoner yet, of my husband's jealousy,

That masters him as he doth master me.

TRULY KIDMAN: I'll tell him how you wish it and wear my
wits to the bone.

MR LITTLEDICK comes back in to the study.

MR LITTLEDICK: What, done so soon? Away, to't again, to't
again, good Sister, to't again; leave her not so. Where left
you? Come!

TRULY KIDMAN: Faith, I am weary, sir.

I cannot draw her from her strict opinion.

Fondly and wilfully she retains that thought,

That every sin is damned.

MR LITTLEDICK: Oh fie, fie, wife! Pea, pea, pea, pea!

There's a diabolical opinion indeed.

Your only deadly sin's Adultery,

That villanous ring-worm.

'Tis only lechery that's dambed to'th hot-hole;

Ah, that's an arch-offence, believe it,

All sins are venial but venereal.

Come hither, lady,

I will not altogether rest ingrateful,

For thy pains and council.

Slip this quietly into your offering box.

TRULY KIDMAN: You do so ravish me with kindness sir.

You virtually make me moist – *(Aside.)* What a Berk.

I'm constrained to take your offering sir,

It's useful in my missionary work

Exit TRULY KIDMAN.

MR LITTLEDICK: Wife, as thou lov'st the quiet of my breast,

Embrace her counsel, yield to her advices;

Thou wilt find comfort in 'em in the end,

Thou'lt feel an alteration; prithee think on't.

Mine eyes can scarce refrain.

MRS LITTLEDICK: Keep in your dew, sir, least when you need it you want it.

MR LITTLEDICK: I've pawned my credit on't. Ah, didst thou know

The sweet fruit once, thoud'st never let it go.

MRS LITTLEDICK: I promise you, 'tis that I strive to get.

Exit MRS LITTLEDICK.

MR LITTLEDICK: Who would not wed? The most delicious life!

No joys are like the comforts of a wife.

2.1

The home of SIR BOUNTEOUS PEERSUCKER.

SIR BOUNTEOUS and his pals have been partying for a great many hours. Young ladies and old men lurch about in varying states of undress. Everyone is just leaving…

SIR ANDREW SKUNKNODGER: Good Sir Bounteous! You have been too much like your name.

SIR BOUNTEOUS: Oh not so, good Knights, not so, you know my humour –

SIR AQUITAINE SQUODGE: Sir Bounteous, will you go to Pimlico with us? We are making a boon voyage to that nappy land of spice-cakes.

SIR BOUNTEOUS: Alas, no. But most welcome good Sir Andrew Skunknodger, Sir Aquitaine Squodge, most welcome.

BOTH: Thanks, good Sir Bounteous.

Exeunt KNIGHTS. Enter OBOE, dressed as a Footman, with false moustache.

FOOTMAN (OBOE): Oh, cry your worship heartily mercy, sir.

SIR BOUNTEOUS: How now, whose footman art thou?

FOOTMAN (OBOE): Pray, can your worship tell me if my lord be come in yet?

SIR BOUNTEOUS: Thy lord! What's his name?

FOOTMAN (OBOE): My Lord Owemuch, Sir. Have you heard of him?

SIR BOUNTEOUS: Heard of him? Why, man, he that has lost both his ears may hear of him. He hath been in great demand of late with our city bankers.

FOOTMAN (OBOE): And is still, sir.

SIR BOUNTEOUS: Much fine rumour have I heard of that lord, yet had I never the fortune to set eye upon him. Art sure he will alight here, footman, the party's over? I am afraid thou'rt mistook.

FOOTMAN (OBOE): Thinks your worship so, sir? *(Going.)* By your leave, sir.

SIR BOUNTEOUS: Puh! Passion of me, footman! Why, pumps, I say, come back.

FOOTMAN (OBOE): Does your worship call?

SIR BOUNTEOUS: Come hither, I say. Did he name the house with the great turret a'th'top?

FOOTMAN (OBOE): No, faith, did he not, sir. *(Going.)*

SIR BOUNTEOUS: Come again you lousy pillicock.

FOOTMAN (OBOE): I beseech, your worship, detain me not.

SIR BOUNTEOUS: Was there no talk of a fair pair of organs, a great gilt candlestick and a pair of silver snuffers?

FOOTMAN (OBOE): T'were sin to belie my Lord, I heard no such words, sir. *(Going.)*

SIR BOUNTEOUS: Was there no speech of a long dining room, a huge kitchen and plentiful portions of pork?

FOOTMAN (OBOE): No, sir.

SIR BOUNTEOUS: Whom did he name?

FOOTMAN (OBOE): Why, one Sir Bounteous Peersucker.

SIR BOUNTEOUS: Ah, a, a, I am that Sir Bounteous you roundabout rascal! I knew I should have him i'th end. There's not a lord will miss me! I warrant ye, there's not one knight i'the'shire able to entertain a cocksure lord or meat-hungry lady like me. There's a kind of grace belongs to't. A kind of Art which naturally slips from me, I know not on't, I promise you. It just squirts out of me. Cuds me, I forget myself... Hello?

Enter SERVANTS.

FIRST SERVANT: Does your worship call?

SIR BOUNTEOUS: Run, sirrah, call in my chief gentleman; expedite.

Exit FIRST SERVANT.

SIR BOUNTEOUS: *(To OBOE/FOOTMAN.)* And how does my good Lord Owemuch? I never saw him before in my life. Bastard!

FOOTMAN (OBOE): Sir?

SIR BOUNTEOUS: Bastard!

FOOTMAN (OBOE): He's always been good to me, sir.

SIR BOUNTEOUS: No, a flagon of bastard, or a cup o'sack to strengthen your wit. The footman's a fool… Spunky! Oh, Spunky!

Enter MASTER SPUNKY.

SIR BOUNTEOUS: Come hither Spunky, come hither. Send presently to Master Pheasant for one of his hens. There's partrige i'th house.

SPUNKY: And woodcock an't please your worship.

SIR BOUNTEOUS: And woodcock an't please thy worship.

SPUNKY: And woodcock an't please your worship.

SIR BOUNTEOUS: I just said that. Remember the pheasant, down with some plover, clap down six woodcocks, my Lord Owemuch is about to come. Let us revel!

SPUNKY: An't please your worship, there's a Lord Owemuch and his followers newly alighted.

SIR BOUNTEOUS: Dispatch I say, dispatch! Why, where's my music? He's come already!

Enter FOLLYWIT in a fine Italian suit and false moustache. SPONGER plays his butler, also with moustache, pulling a large trunk.

SPONGER: Here, sir?

FOLLYWIT: Thank you, Ballbag… Footman.

FOOTMAN (OBOE): My Lord.

FOLLYWIT: Run swiftly with my commendations to Sir Jasper Goldscrote. We'll ride and visit him i'th morning say.

FOOTMAN (OBOE): Your lordship's charge shall be effected.

Exit.

SPUNKY: Your Lordship. *(Exit.)*

FOLLYWIT: That courtly, comely form should present to me Sir Bounteous Peersucker.

SIR BOUNTEOUS: Y'ave found me out, my lord; I cannot hide myself. Your honour is most spaciously welcome.

FOLLYWIT: In this forgive me, sir,
That being a stranger to your houses and you,
I make my way so bold, and presume
Rather upon your kindness than your knowledge,
Only your bounteous disposition
Fame hath divulged, and is to me well known.

SIR BOUNTEOUS: Nay, he you that knows my disposition knows me better than they that know my person. Your honour is so much the welcomer for that.

FOLLYWIT: Thanks, good Sir Bounteous.

SIR BOUNTEOUS: Has your lordship ne'er heard of my organs?

FOLLYWIT: Heard of 'em on my travels, Sir Bounteous, but never heard 'em.

SIR BOUNTEOUS: Your lordship has been a traveller?

FOLLYWIT: Some five year, sir.

SIR BOUNTEOUS: Cuds, 'tis just like my nephew. I confess I love him, and when I die I'll do somewhat for him. But a wild lad he has been.

FOLLYWIT: So we have been all, sir.

SIR BOUNTEOUS: So we have been all indeed, my lord. But I'll pawn my credit for him – never did blaspheme, never came home drunk – an honest trusty bosom.

FOLLYWIT: And that's worth all, sir.

SIR BOUNTEOUS: And that's worth all indeed, my lord. But as long as I live the whoreson boy shall not see his uncle's valuables.

FOLLYWIT: Pardon? Oh… Where do you keep them?

SIR BOUNTEOUS: I keep them in an outlandish place.

SIR BOUNTEOUS activates a mechanism – by tugging on the penis of a Greek statue – that reveals a safe behind a bookcase. He shuts it again by tweaking the statue's nipple.

SIR BOUNTEOUS: But can I be bold with your honour, and suggest this boy hold a plate under your lordship's cup?

FOLLYWIT: Me? Look after your nephew? Very well, for your sake and his I'll reserve a place for him next to my bosom. I swear I shan't be parted from him.

SIR BOUNTEOUS: My good lordship, a thousand thanks. There is no more honest lord than good Lord Owemuch. Come! My music! Give my lord a taste of his welcome.

Music plays and SIR BOUNTEOUS starts to dance. He grabs FOLLYWIT and forces him to dance.

SIR BOUNTEOUS: So, how like you our airs, my Lord? Are they choice?

FOLLYWIT: They're seldom matched, believe it.

SIR BOUNTEOUS: *(Indicates the band.)*
The consort of mine own household.

FOLLYWIT: Yea, sir.

SIR BOUNTEOUS: And your Lordship shall hear my organs now.

FOLLYWIT: Oh, I beseech you Sir Bounteous!

SONG: *'LET THE GOOD TIMES ROLL'* by Sam Theard and Fleecie Moore

2.2

FOLLYWIT as 'LORD OWEMUCH', and his fellows are dressed in pyjamas and dressing gowns. SIR BOUNTEOUS is showing them to their room.

SIR BOUNTEOUS: Silken rest, harmonious slumbers, and venereal dreams to your lordship!

FOLLYWIT: The like to kind Sir Bounteous.

SIR BOUNTEOUS: Fie, not to me my lord. I'm old, past dreaming of such vanities. But tomorrow your lordship shall see my cock, my hens, tickle my trout and make merry in my champion grounds.

FOLLYWIT: Sir Bounteous you o'erwhelm me with delights.

SIR BOUNTEOUS: Once again a musical night to your honour; I'll trouble your lordship no more.

FOLLYWIT: Good rest, Sir Bounteous.

Exit SIR BOUNTEOUS.

FOLLYWIT: So, come, our masks, where be our disguises?

SPONGER: In your lordship's portmanteau.

Meanwhile…

2.3

TRULY KIDMAN has just finished servicing a client. It's the cheap PRIVATE DETECTIVE we saw at MR LITTLEDICK's. He pays her, but she pays him back some of the money immediately.

TRULY KIDMAN: After, sir, run presently to Mr Penitent
Brothel; you know his lodging, knock him up. I know he cannot sleep for sighing.
Tell him I've happily bethought a plan
To make his purpose prosper in each limb,
Which only rests to be approved by him.
Make haste, I know he thirsts for't.

He does so…

2.4

The home of SIR BOUNTEOUS, FOLLYWIT now in full disguise with mask. OBOE and SPONGER are filling the portmanteau with valuables…

FOLLYWIT: The plot's ripe. Come, to our business lads; though guilt condemns, 'tis gilt must make us glad.
Now, uncle, you that hold me at hard meat,

And keep me out at the dag's end, I'll fit you.
Under Lord Owemuch's leave, all must be mine,
He and his will confesses. What I take then
Is but a borrowing of so much beforehand.
Let sires and grandsires keep us low, we must
Live when they're flesh as well as when they're dust.

Enter SPUNKY.

SPUNKY: Oh, oh, oh, thieves, thieves!

FOLLYWIT hits SPUNKY, knocking him out.

FOLLYWIT: Gag that gaping rascal. I'll have no pity of him. How now, lads?

SPONGER: All's sure and safe, the servants are gone to ground.

FOLLYWIT: There's one care past then. Come follow me lads, I'll lead you now to'th'point and top of all your fortunes.

FOLLYWIT tries to activate the mechanism that reveals the safe, but it doesn't work…

SPONGER: So, so, lead on, on.

OBOE: Here's a captain worth the following, and a wit worth a man's love and admiring!

Enter SIR BOUNTEOUS in his nightgown.

SIR BOUNTEOUS: Oh, thieves!

FOLLYWIT and cohorts freeze for a second, look at SIR BOUNTEOUS, then continue with the robbery.

SIR BOUNTEOUS: But kind thieves I'm sure, what countrymen are you?

FOLLYWIT: *(In thick Newcastle accent.)* Of Northumberland, sir.

SPONGER: Why ai man.

OBOE: Pet.

SIR BOUNTEOUS: I am glad of that, i'faith.

FOLLYWIT: And why should you be glad of that?

SIR BOUNTEOUS: Oh, the honestest thieves of all come out of Northumberland, the kindest natured gentlemen; they'll rob a man with conscience. They have a feeling of what they go about, and will steal with tears in their eyes. Ah, pitiful gentlemen.

FOLLYWIT: Push! Money, money, we come for money!

SIR BOUNTEOUS: Is that all you come for? Ah, what a beast was I to put out my money t'other day. Pray come again another time.

FOLLYWIT: Tut, tut, sir, money.

SIR BOUNTEOUS: Oh, not so loud, sir, you're too shrill a gentleman. I have a lord lies in my house.

FOLLYWIT: Who, my Lord Owemuch? He lies bound in his bed, and all his followers.

SIR BOUNTEOUS: Who, my lord? Bound, my lord? Alas, what did you mean to bind my lord? He could keep his bed well enough without binding.

FOLLYWIT: *(Returns to fiddling with the mechanism.)* What is the trick, come!

SIR BOUNTEOUS: *(SIR BOUNTEOUS triggers the mechanism.)* Y'ave undone me already, you need rob me no farther.

They empty the safe and put all in the trunk.

SIR BOUNTEOUS: So, take enough, my masters. My name's Sir Bounteous, what knight but I keep open house at midnight? Well, there should be a moral, if one could hit upon't.

FOLLYWIT: Away now, sieze upon him, bind him!

SIR BOUNTEOUS: Yes, come, come, bind me, I have need on't; I have been too liberal tonight. Keep in my hands; nay, as hard as you like. And I bid you all to dinner tomorrow.

FOLLYWIT: Oh ho, sir!

SIR BOUNTEOUS: Pray, meddle not with my organs, you'll put 'em out of tune.

FOLLYWIT: Oh no, here's better music, sir.

He kicks SIR BOUNTEOUS in the balls.

SIR BOUNTEOUS: Ahhhhg, pox feast you!

FOLLYWIT: Dispatch with him, away!

Exeunt SPONGER and OBOE carrying SIR BOUNTEOUS.

FOLLYWIT: So, thank you, good uncle. Though it came somewhat hard from him at first; for indeed nothing comes stiff from an old man but money. I think one mind runs through a million of 'em; they love to keep us sober all the while they're alive, that when they're dead we may drink to their healths, and that's why so many laugh at their fathers' funerals.

SPONGER and OBOE return.

FOLLYWIT: And we now arrive at the most ticklish point: to be thieves tonight but gentlemen i'th'morning. So look to't lads, it concerns every man's gullet. You know what follows now; one villain binds his fellows. Go, we must be all bound for our own securities. There is a lord to be found bound in the morning, and all his followers.

SPONGER: Oh, admirable spirit!

OBOE: But if we bind one another, how shall the last man be bound?

FOLLYWIT: Pox on't, I'll have Lord Owemuch's footman escape.

OBOE: Lord Owemuch's footman… But that's I! I shall 'scape! I shall 'scape!

FOLLYWIT: Ay, but there must be signs of a struggle!…

He knocks OBOE out with a punch… They start to tie each other up…

2.5

At the Kidman house. TRULY KIDMAN opens the door.

TRULY KIDMAN: Oh, Mr Penitent Brothel!

BROTHEL: Shh, What is't, sweet Miss Kidman that so seizes thee with rapture and admiration?

TRULY KIDMAN: A thought, a trick, to make you, sir, especially happy. You love Mrs Littledick, which no invented means can crown with freedom, but this, which in my 'slumbers' did present itself.

BROTHEL: I'm covetous, lady.

TRULY KIDMAN: You know her husband, ling'ring in suspect, locks her from all society but mine.

BROTHEL: Most true.

TRULY KIDMAN: I only am admitted, yet hitherto that has done you no real happiness; by my admittance I cannot perform that deed that should please you. Wherefore thus I've conveyed it, I'll counterfeit a fit of violent sickness and take to my bed.

BROTHEL: Good, but would it be probable enough to have a sickness so suddenly violent?

TRULY KIDMAN: Puh, all the world knows how easily a woman is put on her back. We can be sick when we have a mind to't, catch cold with the wind of our fans and surfeit upon the rump of a lark. 'Tis the easiest art and cunning for our sex to counterfeit all. We that are always full of fits when we are well. I thus translated into a sick Irish nun, and yourself slipped into the form of a physician –

BROTHEL: I, a physician, lady? Talk not on't, I beseech you. I shall shame the whole college.

TRULY KIDMAN: Tut man, any quacksalving terms will serve for this purpose. 'Tis the ready means for you to have my lady Littledick.

BROTHEL: Yes but, take me with you lady, how, but…

TRULY KIDMAN: To make Mrs Littledick, by the visiting of me, be present to your mutual desire.

BROTHEL: I applaud thee, kiss thee, and will prepare now for my performance.

BROTHEL exits. TRULY KIDMAN sings…

SONG: *'AIN'T NOBODY'S BUSINESS'*
by Porter Grainger and Everett Robbins

2.6

In the Morning. FOLLYWIT's bedchamber at the home of SIR BOUNTEOUS.

FOLLYWIT is tied up and cowering beneath his bedsheets. Enter SIR BOUNTEOUS, hopping, tied up, and in his dressing gown.

SIR BOUNTEOUS: Spunky! Spunky! Ho, Spunky!

FOLLYWIT: *(Feigning terror.)* Ahhh! Ballbag!

SIR BOUNTEOUS: Spunky, come hither!

FOLLYWIT: Agh! Footman, come quick!

SIR BOUNTEOUS: Spunky!

Enter OBOE, dressed once again as a footman.

FOOTMAN (OBOE): *(To SIR BOUNTEOUS.)* Oh, good your worship, your good old worship.

SIR BOUNTEOUS: Ah, poor honest footman, how didst thou 'scape this massacre?

FOOTMAN (OBOE): 'Tis a miracle, sir!

SIR BOUNTEOUS: I think so. But the binding of my lord cuts my heart in two pieces; so, so, run to thy fellows, undo 'em, undo 'em, undo 'em.

FOOTMAN (OBOE): All right, all right, all right…

OBOE runs out, wailing.

SIR BOUNTEOUS: If I be not ashamed to look my lord i'th'face I'm a Muslim. My lord –

FOLLYWIT: Who's that?

SIR BOUNTEOUS: One may see he has been scarred; a pox on 'em for their labours.

FOLLYWIT: Is't you, Ballbag?! Who's that i'th chamber?

SIR BOUNTEOUS: Good morrow my lord, 'tis I.

He pulls back the sheets.

FOLLYWIT: Sir Bounteous, good morrow. I would give you my hand sir, but I cannot come at it. Is this the courtesy o'th country, Sir Bounteous?

SIR BOUNTEOUS: Your Lordship grieves me more than all my loss;

'Tis the unnatural'st sight that can be found,

To see a noble gentleman hard bound.

FOLLYWIT: Trust me, I thought you had been better belov'd, Sir Bounteous; but I see you have enemies, sir, and your friends fare the worse for 'em. I like your talk better than your lodging. Can you not guess what they should be, Sir Bounteous?

SIR BOUNTEOUS: Faith, Northumberland men, my Lord.

FOLLYWIT: Believe it not, sir. These are local men feigning terrible Northumberland accents, I warrant you.

SIR BOUNTEOUS: Think you so, my Lord?

FOLLYWIT: They know your house, sir, and are familiar with all the conveniences.

SIR BOUNTEOUS: This is the commodity of keeping open house, my lord, that makes so many shut their doors about dinner time.

FOLLYWIT: I made myself known to 'em, told 'em what I was; gave 'em my honourable word not to disclose 'em. But they told me posh promises were mortal, and commonly die within half an hour after they are spoken.

SIR BOUNTEOUS: Saucy, unmannerly villains!

FOLLYWIT: Troth, I'm of that mind, Sir Bounteous. You fared the worse for my coming hither.

SIR BOUNTEOUS: Ah good my Lord, but I'm sure your Lordship fared the worse.

FOLLYWIT: Pray, pity not me, sir.

SIR BOUNTEOUS: Is not your honour sore about the brawn of the arm? You feel, as it were, a twinge, my lord?

FOLLYWIT: Ay, e'en a twinge; you say right.

SIR BOUNTEOUS: A pox discover 'em, that twinge I feel too.

FOLLYWIT: But that which disturbs me most, Sir Bounteous, lies here.

SIR BOUNTEOUS: True, about the wrist a kind of tumid numbness.

FOLLYWIT: You say true, Sir.

SIR BOUNTEOUS: The reason of that, my lord, is the pulses had no play.

FOLLYWIT: Mass, so I guessed it.

SIR BOUNTEOUS: A mischief swell 'em, for I feel that too.

Enter SPONGER dressed as 'BALLBAG'.

SPONGER: God's eyelid, here's a house haunted indeed.

SIR BOUNTEOUS: A word with you, sir.

FOLLYWIT: How now, Ballbag?

SPONGER: I'm sorry, my lord, but your Lord Owemuch has lost –

SIR BOUNTEOUS: Pup, pup, pup, pup, pup!

FOLLYWIT: What have I lost? Speak.

SIR BOUNTEOUS: *(Aside, to SPONGER.)* A good night's sleep, say.

FOLLYWIT: Speak, what have I lost, I say?

SPONGER: A good night's sleep, my lord, nothing else.

FOLLYWIT: That's true. My clothes, come!

SPONGER: My lord's clothes! His honour's rising!

Enter OBOE with clothes. As FOLLYWIT is dressed, SIR BOUNTEOUS takes BALLBAG (SPONGER) to one side.

SIR BOUNTEOUS: Hist, well said. Come hither; what has my Lord lost? Tell me. Speak softly.

SPONGER: 'Twill do you no pleasure to know't, sir.

SIR BOUNTEOUS: Ssh! I desire it, I say.

SPONGER: Since your worship will needs know't, they have stolen away a jewel in a blue silk ribbon of a hundred pound price, beside some hundred pounds in money.

SIR BOUNTEOUS: But that's some two hundred and fifty in total!

SPONGER: Not much gets past you, sir.

SIR BOUNTEOUS: Come, follow me; I'll make that whole again in so much money.

3.1

MASTER MUCHLY-MINTED and MASTER WHOPPING-PROSPECT have just arrived at the home of MR LITTLEDICK.

MR LITTLEDICK: You're kindly welcome to my house, good Master Muchly-Minted and Master Whopping-Prospect .

MASTER WHOPPING-PROSPECT: Mr Littledick.

MASTER MUCHLY-MINTED: We're honoured to be invited, sir.

MR LITTLEDICK: Hello?!

DETECTIVE: *(Enters.)* Here, sir.

MR LITTLEDICK: Call down my mistress to welcome these two gentlemen, my friends.

DETECTIVE: I shall, sir.

Exits.

MR LITTLEDICK: *(To himself, obsessed.)*
Now in the presence of these gentlemen
I will observe her carriage and watch
The slippery revolutions of her eye;
I'll lie in wait for every glance she gives,
And weigh her words i'th'balance of suspicion;
If she but sways, either on this hand
Over familiar, or this, too neglectful,
She's gone!

MASTER WHOPPING-PROSPECT: But Master Littledick.

MR LITTLEDICK: True, I hear you, sir; was't you said?

MASTER WHOPPING-PROSPECT: I have not spoke it yet, sir.

MR LITTLEDICK: Right, so I say.

MASTER WHOPPING-PROSPECT: Is it not strange, that in so short a time, my little Miss Kidman should be so violently ill?

MR LITTLEDICK: Oh, sickness has no mercy, sir. It crops the rose out of the virgin's cheek and so deflowers her that was ne'er deflowered. And though I hide it, that sweet virgin's sickness grieves me not lightly; she was my wife's only delight and company; I'th'midst of her extremest fit, she called out for my wife, sweet Mistress Littledick? And, when she sent for me, o' one side of her bed stood a sort of physician, the scrivener o'th'other, fashioning her will, and she did instruct me that her best and richest jewel she would fain give as a legacy unto my wife – in person. She was most insistent I'faith and so of all others my wife has most reason to visit her.

Enter DETECTIVE.

MR LITTLEDICK: Now, sir, where's my wife?

DETECTIVE: She desires you and the gentlemen friends to
    hold her excused; sh'as a fever now upon her which begins
    to shake her.

MR LITTLEDICK: Oh? Is she ill too? Where does it shake her
    most?

DETECTIVE: All over her body, sir.

MR LITTLEDICK: Shake all her body? 'Tis a saucy fit; I'm
    jealous of that fever. Pray, leave us, gentlemen. This is very
    bad.

MASTER WHOPPING-PROSPECT: Of course, Mister Littledick.

MASTER MUCHLY-MINTED: Our thoughts be with your wife.

They leave.

DETECTIVE: Now they are absent, sir, 'tis no such thing.

MR LITTLEDICK: What?

DETECTIVE: Your mistress has her health, sir,
    But 'tis her suit she may confine herself
    From sight of all men but your own dear self, sir,
    For since the sickness of that modest virgin,
    Miss Kidman, her only company, she delights in none.

MR LITTLEDICK: No? Visit her again, commend me to her,
    Tell her they're gone and only I myself
    Walk here to exchange a word or two with her.

DETECTIVE: I'll tell her so, sir.

Exit.

MR LITTLEDICK: Fool that I am, and madman, beast! What
    worse?
    Suspicion o'er a creature that deserves
    The best opinion and the purest thought;
    Watchful o'er her that is her watch herself;
    To doubt her ways that looks too narrowly

Into her own defects. I, foolish-fearful
Have often rudely, out of giddy flames,
Barred her those objects which she shuns herself.
Ah, let me curse myself, that could be jealous
Of her whose mind no sin can make rebellious.
And here the unmatched comes –

Enter MRS LITTLEDICK.

MRS LITTLEDICK: Husband? Are the men gone?

MR LITTLEDICK: Now, wife, i'faith they're gone.
Push, see how fearful 'tis! They are gone i'faith, think you
I'll betray you? Come, come, thy delight and mine, thy
only virtuous friend, thy sweet instructress is now violently
ill, grievous sick, and which is worse, she mends not. She
calls still upon thee, poor soul, remembers thee still, thy
name whirls in her breath. 'Where's Mistress Littledick?'
says she?

MRS LITTLEDICK: E'en to the last gasp a kind soul.

MR LITTLEDICK: Take my man. Go, visit her.

MRS LITTLEDICK: Man? I would not take your man, sir,
though I did purpose going.

MR LITTLEDICK: No? Still she holds the same rare temper.
Thy reason?

MRS LITTLEDICK: The world's condition is itself so vile, sir,
'Tis apt to judge the worst of those deserve not.
This censure flies from one, that from another,
That man's her squire, says he; her pimp, t'other;
She's easy meat, a third; fourth, I have had her.
I've heard this not without a burning cheek.
Then our attires are looked on, our very gait
Is called in question, where a husband's presence
Scatters such thoughts, or makes 'em sink for fear
Into the hearts that breed 'em.

MR LITTLEDICK: With me or no man, incomparable such a woman.

MRS LITTLEDICK: Nay, surely,
If I went, sir, I would entreat your company.

MR LITTLEDICK: Mine? Prithee, wife, I have been there already.

MRS LITTLEDICK: That's all one; although you bring me but to'th'door, sir, I would intreat no farther.

MR LITTLEDICK: Th'art such a wife; why I will bring thee right to'th'door, but not penetrate within.

MRS LITTLEDICK: I'faith you shall not; I do not desire it, sir.

MR LITTLEDICK: Why then, content.

MRS LITTLEDICK: Give me your hand you will do so, sir.

MR LITTLEDICK: Why here's my lip I will!

MRS LITTLEDICK: *(Ignores his offer of a kiss.)* Why, then I go, sir.

Exit.

MR LITTLEDICK sings…

SONG: *'PLEASE LOVE ME'*
by Riley B King and Jules Bihari

3.2

TRULY KIDMAN is in bed practising for her performance as a very ill woman. PENITENT BROTHEL enters, dressed up as a doctor.

BROTHEL: Lady?

TRULY KIDMAN: Ha, what news? Is Mistress Littledick here?

BROTHEL: No, but there's one Sir Bounteous Peersucker newly arrived.

TRULY KIDMAN: God's eyelid, 'tis the knight that privately maintains me; my meat, drink and raiment – let us pump him for money.

BROTHEL: What?!

TRULY KIDMAN: 'Tis easy – many's the time and often he's blown his wad on me.

BROTHEL: But I know him and him me.

TRULY KIDMAN: Be my good physician. Let gold amber and desolved pearl be common ingredients. Tell him you cannot make a medicine without 'em, and rack up the reckoning. Put but cunningly in practice and it shall be sufficient recompense for all my pains.

BROTHEL: What?!

TRULY KIDMAN: Squeeze his pockets, I'll be weak.

SIR BOUNTEOUS enters.

SIR BOUNTEOUS: Why, where be these ladies, these plump, soft, delicate creatures, ha?! Gather up a good spirit wench. I'm the cook here to bone the chicken.

BROTHEL: Who would you visit, sir?

SIR BOUNTEOUS: What are you with the plague in your mouth? Another suitor?

BROTHEL: A physician, sir. Cigarette?

TRULY KIDMAN: Ah, Sir Bounteous…!

SIR BOUNTEOUS: How now? What art thou?

TRULY KIDMAN: I am very weak, truly; have not eaten so much as the bulk of an egg these three days.

SIR BOUNTEOUS: Passion of me, what an alteration's here! Here's a sight able to make an old man shrink. I was lusty when I came in, but I am down now i'faith. Mortality! Yea, this puts me in mind of another hole seven-foot deep, my grave, my grave, my grave. Hist, Master Doctor, 'tis not the plague, is't?

BROTHEL: The plague, sir? No!

SIR BOUNTEOUS: Thank God for that!

BROTHEL: *(Aside.)* He ne'er asks whether it be the clap or no, and of the twain that had been more likely.

SIR BOUNTEOUS: How now my wench? How dost?

TRULY KIDMAN: *(Coughs.)* Huh – weak, knight – huh…

SIR BOUNTEOUS: What could it be? – Ha! – Perhaps I have got thee with child i'faith?

TRULY KIDMAN: Yes, and I never thought you could give me one.

SIR BOUNTEOUS: Oh, could it be true?! Proud at last! A young Peersucker when all's done.

TRULY KIDMAN: Who would have thought it possible, sir.

SIR BOUNTEOUS: I see by her 'tis nothing but a surfeit of Venus i'faith, and though I be old, I have gin't her. But since I had the power to make thee sick, I'll have the purse to make thee whole, that's certain. Master Doctor.

BROTHEL: Sir.

SIR BOUNTEOUS: Let's hear, I pray, what i'st you minister to her?

BROTHEL: Marry, sir, a precious cordial, a costly compound both comfortable and restorative.

SIR BOUNTEOUS: Ay, ay, that, that, that.

BROTHEL: No poorer ingredients then the liquor of coral, clear amber, horn of unicorn, fermented monkey glands and milk-thistle.

SIR BOUNTEOUS: Ay! Ay!

BROTHEL: Osso bucco, tortellini, mellenzane parmigiane…

SIR BOUNTEOUS: Very precious, sir.

BROTHEL: All which being finely mashed and mixed in a mortar of stone… *(TRULY KIDMAN coughs.)* …or diamond, together with the spirit of waspfart. It takes time, Sir.

SIR BOUNTEOUS: Then we shall be patient, Sir.

BROTHEL: That's impossible, I cannot be patient and physician too, Sir.

SIR BOUNTEOUS: Oh, cry you mercy, that's true, Sir!

BROTHEL: And at last, when 'tis well-mashed I add thereto some pannatone, some cinnamoni and half a pint of Guinness.

SIR BOUNTEOUS: Well, be of good cheer wench, there's more gold for thee. Huh, let her want for nothing, Master Doctor. A poor kinswoman of mine; nature binds me to have a care of her. *(Aside.)* I have fooled thee there Master Doctor! Ha ha, I have sorted her out, an old knight and a cock o'th game still! *(To BROTHEL.)* Take good care of her Master Doctor – I already have!

Exits.

TRULY KIDMAN: Is he gone?

BROTHEL: He's like himself. Gone.

TRULY KIDMAN: He only fears he has done that deed which I ne'er feared to come from him in my life. How soon he took occasion to slip in to his own flattery, *(She holds up the money.)* – and behold, his heirs!

BROTHEL: Hist, a pair of forward young gentlemen.

TRULY KIDMAN: Oh, they're welcome, they bring money too.

BROTHEL: But…

TRULY KIDMAN: Think on't. A brace of elder brothers new perfumed in the first of their fortunes. We shall see how forward their purses will be to the restoring of my health.

BROTHEL: But 'tis the appointed hour for my sweet Mrs Littledick.

TRULY KIDMAN: Push. Open the door.

BROTHEL: Gentlemen!

Enter MASTER MUCHLY-MINTED and MASTER WHOPPING-PROSPECT.

46

MASTER WHOPPING-PROSPECT: Master Doctor, how does she now?

BROTHEL: Faith, after one fashion, sir.

MASTER MUCHLY-MINTED: There's hope of life, sir?

BROTHEL: I see no signs of death of her.

MASTER WHOPPING-PROSPECT: That's some comfort. Will she take anything?

BROTHEL: Yes, yes, yes, she'll take still. She has a kind of facility in taking.

MASTER WHOPPING-PROSPECT: Lady, how cheer you now?

TRULY KIDMAN: The same woman still; little alteration. 'Tis the way of cheap physic.

MASTER WHOPPING-PROSPECT: Then take the fruit of my bulging pockets.

They hand over some money.

TRULY KIDMAN: Fie, fie, you have been too lavish, gentlemen.

MASTER MUCHLY-MINTED: Puh, talk not of that, lady. Thy health's worth a million. Here, Master Doctor, spare for no cost.

MASTER WHOPPING-PROSPECT: *(Hands over more money.)* Look what you find there, sir.

TRULY KIDMAN: Put it away, put it away! You have me on my back, sweaty and helpless, I would not take it else. But if I ever live I will pay back in the currency of your deepest desire.

MASTER WHOPPING-PROSPECT: Mistress Littledick, lady, is setting forth presently to visit you too.

TRULY KIDMAN: What! Now! Really?

BROTHEL: *(Aside.)* There struck the minute that brings forth the birth of all my joys and wishes. But see the rub now! How shall I rid these from her? A word with you, gentlemen.

MASTERS MUCHLY-MINTED
AND WHOPPING-PROSPECT: What says, Master Doctor?

BROTHEL: She wants but settling of her sense with rest. One hour's sleep, gentlemen, would set all parts in tune.

MASTER WHOPPING-PROSPECT: He says true, i'faith.

MASTER MUCHLY-MINTED: Get her to sleep, Master Doctor. We'll both sit here and watch by her.

BROTHEL: *(Aside.)* Hell's Angels watch you! No art can prevail with 'em. My wits are spread as wide as a jezebel's legs!

TRULY KIDMAN: Master Doctor, Master Doctor?

BROTHEL: Here, lady.

TRULY KIDMAN: The waspfart works its magic, bring me a bedpan!

PENITENT BROTHEL fetches a bedpan and places it under her. She appears to defecate copiously.

MASTER WHOPPING-PROSPECT: Farewell, sweet lady.

MASTER MUCHLY-MINTED: Adieu, Master Doctor.

They leave.

TRULY KIDMAN: So.

BROTHEL: Let me admire thee,
The wit of man wanes and decreases soon,
But women's wit is ever at full moon.

Enter MRS LITTLEDICK.

BROTHEL: There shot a star from heaven; I dare not yet behold my happiness.
The splendour is so glorious and so piercing.

TRULY KIDMAN: Mistress Littledick, give my wit thanks hereafter. Your wishes are in sight, your opportunity spacious.

MRS LITTLEDICK: Will you but hear a word from me?

TRULY KIDMAN: What, why?!

MRS LITTLEDICK: My husband himself brought me to the door, and now walks above for my return; jealousy is prick-eared, and would hear the pruning of a bush.

TRULY KIDMAN: Pish, y'are a lily-liver. Trust yourself with your pleasure, and me with your security; go!

BROTHEL: The fullness of my wish!

MRS LITTLEDICK: Of my desire!

BROTHEL: Beyond this sphere I never will aspire.

TRULY KIDMAN: Hang virginity upon the pole of carnality!

BROTHEL and MRS LITTLEDICK pull the curtains of the four poster closed. MR LITTLEDICK is listening through the floor of the room above. BROTHEL and MRS LITTLEDICK's lovemaking can soon be heard. TRULY KIDMAN invents to cover their noise...

MR LITTLEDICK: I'll listen now this woman's flesh draws near the end.

MRS LITTLEDICK: Ahhh!

MR LITTLEDICK: At such a time women exchange their secrets
And ransack the close corners of their hearts;
What many years hath stopped, this hour imparts.

TRULY KIDMAN: Pray, sit down, there's a chair, good Mistress Littledick, this was kindly done.

MRS LITTLEDICK: Huh!

TRULY KIDMAN: Give me your hand.

MRS LITTLEDICK: Huh!

TRULY KIDMAN: Alas, how cold you are. Even so is your husband, that worthy wise gentleman; a man who only waits…

MRS LITTLEDICK: Huh! Huh!

TRULY KIDMAN: …to satisfy his wife. Love him –

MRS LITTLEDICK: Yes!

TRULY KIDMAN: Honour him –

MRS LITTLEDICK: Yes!

TRULY KIDMAN: Stick by him –

MRS LITTLEDICK: Yes!

TRULY KIDMAN: He lets you want nothing that's fit for a woman –

MRS LITTLEDICK: Yes!

TRULY KIDMAN: And to be sure on't, he will see himself that you –

MRS LITTLEDICK: Yes?

TRULY KIDMAN: …want it not.

MR LITTLEDICK: And so I do, i'faith, 'tis right my humour.

TRULY KIDMAN: You live a lady's life with him, go where you will, ride when you will…

MR LITTLEDICK: Aye – I'll buy a horse i'faith.

MRS LITTLEDICK: Ooooh…! Yes!

TRULY KIDMAN: …and ask for what you will.

MRS LITTLEDICK: Oh my God! I need, I need, I need…

TRULY KIDMAN: I know you do, you need not tell me that.

MRS LITTLEDICK: Aaahh!

TRULY KIDMAN: 'Twere e'en pity of your life i'faith…

MRS LITTLEDICK: Aaahh!

TRULY KIDMAN: …if ever you should wrong such an innocent gentleman.

MRS LITTLEDICK: Ooh-ooh-ooh!

TRULY KIDMAN: Fie, Mistress Littledick, what do you mean?

MRS LITTLEDICK can be heard panting.

TRULY KIDMAN: Come you to discomfort me?

MRS LITTLEDICK lets out a long moan.

TRULY KIDMAN: Nothing but weeping with you?

MR LITTLEDICK: She's weeping, 't'as made her weep. My wife shows her good nature already.

Another moan.

TRULY KIDMAN: Still, still weeping?

MRS LITTLEDICK: Huff, huff, huff…!

TRULY KIDMAN: Why, how now, woman?

MRS LITTLEDICK: Heh, heh…!

TRULY KIDMAN: Hey, what's got into you?

MRS LITTLEDICK: Oh oh…Aaaaaah!

TRULY KIDMAN: She cannot even answer me for wailing.

MR LITTLEDICK: All this does her good. I'll not be her hindrance.

MRS LITTLEDICK: No, no…!

TRULY KIDMAN: No, lay your hand here Mistress Littledick.

MRS LITTLEDICK: I, I…!

TRULY KIDMAN: Ay, there!

MRS LITTLEDICK: There, there…!

TRULY KIDMAN: Yes, there lies my pain good gentlewoman.

MRS LITTLEDICK: Ooooorrr!

TRULY KIDMAN: Sore?

MRS LITTLEDICK: Oh, oh…!

TRULY KIDMAN: Oh, I can scarce endure your hand upon't.

MR LITTLEDICK: Poor soul, how she's tormented.

MRS LITTLEDICK: Yes, yes…!

TRULY KIDMAN: Yes, I had some soup an hour since.

MR LITTLEDICK: There's some comfort in that yet; Miss Kidman may 'scape it.

MRS LITTLEDICK: Oh, oh…!

TRULY KIDMAN: Oh, it lies about my stomach much!

MR LITTLEDICK: I'm sorry for that i'faith; she surely won't 'scape it.

MRS LITTLEDICK: No, no…!

TRULY KIDMAN: No, I had a very comfortable stool this morning.

MR LITTLEDICK: That's a good sign!

MRS LITTLEDICK: Ahhhhh!

TRULY KIDMAN: Will you be going then?

MRS LITTLEDICK: Yes, yes, yes, yes…!

MR LITTLEDICK: Fall back, she's coming.

MRS LITTLEDICK, TRULY KIDMAN & BROTHEL: Yeeeeeeeeessssss!

MR LITTLEDICK: Good. She'll feel better for that.

TRULY KIDMAN: Thanks, good Mistress Littledick; welcome, sweet Mistress Littledick; pray commend me to the good gentleman your husband –

MR LITTLEDICK: I could do that myself now.

MR LITTLEDICK starts to come down from above.

TRULY KIDMAN: And to my uncle Titsfatprick, my cousins Willy and Lickit, my Great Aunty Rugmunch, and to all my relations in and around Soho.

MRS LITTLEDICK and BROTHEL stagger from the bed.

MRS LITTLEDICK: At three days' end my husband takes a journey.

BROTHEL: Oh, thence I derive a second meeting.

MRS LITTLEDICK: May it prosper still,
Till then I rest a captive to his will.
Once again, health, rest, and strength to thee sweet Lady: farewell, you witty squall. Good Master Doctor, have a care to her body; if you stand her friend, I know you can do her good.

TRULY KIDMAN: Take pity of your waiter, go. Farewell, sweet Mistress Littledick.

MR LITTLEDICK bounds into the room.

MR LITTLEDICK: Mistress Littledick, sweet Mrs Littledick. Alight upon my lip. Never was an hour spent better.

MRS LITTLEDICK: Why, were you within the hearing, sir?

MR LITTLEDICK: Ay, that I was i'faith…to my great comfort; I deceived you there, wife, ha, ha!
I do entreat thee, nay conjure thee, wife,
Upon my love, or what can more be said,
Oft'ner to visit this sick, virtuous maid.

MRS LITTLEDICK: Be not so fierce; your will shall be obeyed.

MR LITTLEDICK: Why, then I see thou lov'st me.

Exit all but BROTHEL.

BROTHEL: Art of Ladies!
When plots are e'en past hope, and hang their head,
Set with a woman's hand, they thrive and spread.

Interval.

3.3

Outside The Moka Bar.

FOLLYWIT: Was't not well managed, you necessary mischiefs? Did the plot want either life or Art?

SPONGER: 'Twas so well, captain.

FOLLYWIT: I am sure my uncle ne'er got his money by worse means than I got it from him. If ever he did cheat the simple, I was born to revenge their quarrell; if ever oppress the widow, I, a fatherless child, have done as much for him.

SPONGER: Two hundred pounds in fair rose nobles!

FOLLYWIT: Push, I knew he could not sleep quietly 'til he had paid me for robbing of him too; 'tis his humour and the humour of most of your rich men, they always feast those mouths that are least needy. *(Jumps.)* Oh!

SPONGER: Cuds me, how now, Captain?

FOLLYWIT: A cold fit that comes over my memory and pulls at my fortunes.

SPONGER: What's that, sir?

FOLLYWIT: Is it for certain, Sponger, that my uncle keeps an uncertain creature, a paid mistress, a strumpet, a tart, a puckbunny?

SPONGER: Ay, that's true, sir.

FOLLYWIT: So much the worse for me; she may carry away a third o'th'will. I have known many a game-thirsty father, when his best parts hang down their heads for shame, to fall for his blanched harlot and make the pox his heir. How had'st thou first knowledge on't, Sargent.

SPONGER: Faith, from the town, yet despite all effort I could not get her name.

FOLLYWIT: Dull slave!

SPONGER: But the manner of her coming was describ'd to me.

FOLLYWIT: Oh, how does she come?

SPONGER: She comes with great fanfare, in a coach. Then alighting at your uncle's she's privately received by the butler, Spunky.

FOLLYWIT: The gentleman's gentleman facilitating a gentleman's gentleman.

SPONGER: Then is your uncle told of her arrival, whereupon he takes her round the back way, into his private chamber, there remaining 'til either she gives wood for him for his fire or he has a poke at his own embers.

FOLLYWIT: Peace, I ha't.

SPONGER: Art mad again, sir?

FOLLYWIT: Nay – a man's never at high height of mad moon's misrule,

'Til he walk lovers' lane and prove a woman's fool.

SPONGER: What, then?

FOLLYWIT: My uncle's a woman's fool! – thanks, thanks to any spirit that mingled it 'mongst my inventions!

OBOE: Why, Master Follywit?

FOLLYWIT: Give me scope and hear me.

I have begot a plan which will both endow me
And drive that tart from his affections.

SPONGER: That were double happiness, to put thyself into money and her out of favour.

FOLLYWIT: And all at one dealing?

OBOE: God's foot, I long to see that hand played.

FOLLYWIT: Sargent Sponger, if I mistook not, there hangs the lower part of a gentlewoman's gown and a gentlewoman within it; I'll bring that piece of skirt to myself.

OBOE: But prithee, what wilt thou do with a gentlewoman's lower part?

FOLLYWIT: Why, use it, Private.

FOLLYWIT exit.

SPONGER: I love mad tricks as well as my Dick but we're all male to the middle, mankind from the beaver to the bum.

OBOE: Dick? Bum? Beaver? What is he doing with that woman?

SPONGER: Private Oboe, ever while you live put a woman's clothes over her head, Cupid plays best at blind man's buff.

FOLLYWIT appears dressed as a woman.

SPONGER: Oh, very good. But what shift will you make for upper bodies, captain?

FOLLYWIT: I see now thou'rt an ass. *(Puts two iced buns with cherries on top down his blouse.)* Why, I'm ready!

SPONGER: Ready?

FOLLYWIT: You shall see; we can be whatever we choose. The most musty-visage critic shall not except against me.

SPONGER: Nay, I'll give thee thy due from behind. A kind of Amazonian woman.

FOLLYWIT: 'Tis an Amazonian time. You shall shortly have women tread their husbands.

WAITRESS: Yeah.

FOLLYWIT: Did not I tell you rascals you should see a woman quickly made-up?

OBOE: A woman quickly made-up? Tis a miracle!

FOLLYWIT: Now come, bestir your bones, you ponderous beef-buttocked knaves! Where's the flesh-colour velvet cushion now for my lady's pease-porridge-tawny-satin bum?

SPONGER offers a chair.

FOLLYWIT: Now, let me see; who shall I choose for a pimp
now? But I cannot choose between you, that's the best.
Well, as I am a queen of tarts, you both best have a care of
me, and guard me sure; I give you warning beforehand,
'tis a monkey-tailed age. An age of exploration, where
anything goes. There's not a man here that wouldn't like to
circumnavigate my globes, sail his frigate into my harbour
and fire off a twenty-four gun salute. Oh, they'd polish my
rollocks on the poopdeck and wax my futtocks given half
the chance.

OBOE: I know I would, sir.

FOLLYWIT: Why then, set forward. And as you scorn two-
shilling whores and twelve-penny pimps, guard me from
cheapskate husbands, skinflint students and any man likely
to frequent a common playhouse! Forward!

4.1

*BROTHEL is in his bedsit, frying a chipolata on a hotplate and reading
a grease-spotted religious primer. He begins to whip himself…*

BROTHEL: Ha! Read that place again. 'Adultery
Draws the divorce 'twixt heaven and the soul!'
Accursèd man that stand'st divorced from heaven,
Thou wretched unthrift that hast played away
Thy eternal portion at a minute's game,
To please the flesh hast blotted out thy name.
Where were thy nobler meditations busied
That they durst trust this body with itself,
This natural drunkard that undoes us all
And makes our shame apparent in our fall?
O, that I that knew the price of life and sin
Should dote on weakness, slime, corruption, woman!
What is she, took asunder from her clothes?
Being stripped she consists of one hundred moving parts,
Much like your German clock.
Then let my blood pay for't and vex and boil.

Within these three days the next meeting's fixed;
If I meet then hell and my soul be mixed.
My lodging I know constantly, she not knows.
Sin's hate is the best gift that sin bestows;
I'll ne'er embrace her more; never, bear witness, never.

He sings…

SONG: '*YIELD NOT TO TEMPTATION*' by D Malone

Music continues. He has not noticed the smoke that is pouring from the pan. MRS LITTLEDICK appears through the smoke as if from nowhere.

SUCCUBUS (MRS LITTLEDICK): Ooh, standing to attention the fitter for my company.

BROTHEL: Celestial soldiers guard me –

SUCCUBUS (MRS LITTLEDICK): How now, man? Did the quickness of my presence fright thee?

BROTHEL: Shield me, you ministers of faith and grace.

SUCCUBUS (MRS LITTLEDICK): Are you not ashamed to use such words to a woman?

BROTHEL: Th'art a devil!

SUCCUBUS (MRS LITTLEDICK): A devil? Feel, feel man. Has a devil flesh and bone?

BROTHEL: I do conjure thee by the power of that hellish fire –

SUCCUBUS (MRS LITTLEDICK): The man has a delight to make me tremble.
Are these the fruits of thy adventurous love?
Was I enticed for this? To be soon rejected?
Come, what has changed thee so, delight?

BROTHEL: Away!

SUCCUBUS (MRS LITTLEDICK): Remember –

BROTHEL: Leave my sight!

SUCCUBUS (MRS LITTLEDICK): Have I this meeting wrought with cunning

Which, when I come, I find thee shunning?
Rouse thy amorous thoughts and twine me,
All my depths I here resign thee.
Shall we let slip this mutual hour
Comes so seldom in our power?
Where's thy lip, thy clip, thy pluck?
Let us strip, unzip and… *(He gasps.)*
Art a man? Or dost abuse one?
A love? And know'st not how to use one?
Come, I'll teach thee.

BROTHEL: Do not follow.

SUCCUBUS (MRS LITTLEDICK): Once so firm and now so
    hollow?
When was place and season sweeter?
Thy bliss in sight and dar'st not eat her?
Where's thy courage, youth and vigour?
Love's best pleased when't's seared with rigour;
Sear me then with veins most cheerful,
Women love no flesh that's fearful.
Fa le la, le la, fa le la, la la;
Fa le la, le la, fa le la, la la –

BROTHEL: Torment me not!

SUCCUBUS (MRS LITTLEDICK): Fa le la, le la, fa le la, la la –

BROTHEL: Fury!

SUCCUBUS (MRS LITTLEDICK): Fa le la, fa le la, fa la la loh.

BROTHEL: Devil! I do conjure thee once again
By that soul-quaking thunder to depart
And leave this chamber freed from thy damned art.

*In his terror, BROTHEL has grabbed a tiny domestic fire extinguisher.
He lets it off at her. MRS LITTLEDICK seems to disappear magically
in the smoke.*

BROTHEL: It has prevailed. Oh my sin-shaking sinews! What should I think? What should I think?!

Enter CARETAKER.

CARETAKER: Sir, how now? What has disturbed you, sir?

BROTHEL: A fit, a qualm, is Mistress Littledick gone?

CARETAKER: Who, sir? Mistress Littledick?

BROTHEL: Is she gone. I say?

CARETAKER: Gone? Why, she was never here yet.

BROTHEL: No?

CARETAKER: Why, no, sir.

BROTHEL: Art sure on't?

CARETAKER: Sure on't? If I be sure I breathe and am myself?

BROTHEL: I like it not. Where kept'st thou?

CARETAKER: I'th'hallway, sir.

BROTHEL: Why, she struck by thee, man.

CARETAKER: You'd make one mad, sir; that a gentlewoman should steal by me and I not hear her. God's foot, one may hear the ruffling of their bums almost an hour before we see 'em!

BROTHEL: When men's intents are wicked, their guilt haunts 'em,

But when they're just, they're armed and nothing daunts 'em.

CARETAKER: What strange humour call you this? He dreams of women and both his eyes broad open!

4.2

At the home of SIR BOUNTEOUS.

SIR BOUNTEOUS: How now, Spunky, what news?

SPUNKY: I have a thing to tell your worship –

SIR BOUNTEOUS: Why, prithee, tell me; speak, man.

SPUNKY: Your worship shall pardon me, I have better bringing up than so.

SIR BOUNTEOUS: How, sir?

SPUNKY: 'Tis a delicate matter, sir.

SIR BOUNTEOUS: Oh, oh, oh, cry you mercy, now I begin to taste you! Is she come?

SPUNKY: She's come, sir?

SIR BOUNTEOUS: Recovered, well and sound again?

SPUNKY: That's to be feared, sir.

SIR BOUNTEOUS: Why, sir?

SPUNKY: She wears a scarf about her head.

SIR BOUNTEOUS: Ha, ha! Why that's the fashion, Spunky, you son of a whore!

SPUNKY: Fashion, sir? Live I so long time to see a fashion that in former days was an emblem of dispraise, a sign o'th'clap ridden?

SIR BOUNTEOUS: Ay, ay, in those days, but that was a queasy time. The clap is as natural now as a cold i'th'springtime. These days an old man's appetite is very up and down. One starts with the soup but rarely gets to the nuts. You know your duty.

SPUNKY: I know my office sir.

SIR BOUNTEOUS exits.

4.3

The boudoir of SIR BOUNTEOUS. FOLLYWIT is in full disguise as a high-class call girl. SPUNKY is showing him/her around.

SPUNKY: Come, lady, you know where you are now?

FOLLYWIT: Yes, good sir.

SPUNKY: This is the old closet, you know.

FOLLYWIT: I remember it well, sir.

SPUNKY: There stands the casket. I would my yearly revenue were but worth the wealth thats locked in't, lady; yet I do have fifty pound a year, wench.

SPUNKY dangles the key to the casket on the chain.

FOLLYWIT: Including your chain, sir?

SPUNKY: No, by my troth, that's extra. Faith, if you consider me rightly, sweet lady, you might admit this choice gentleman into your service.

FOLLYWIT: Oh, pray away, sir.

SPUNKY: Pusha, come, come, you do but hinder your fortunes i'faith. I have the command of all the house; I can tell you, nothing comes into'th' kitchen but comes through my hands.

FOLLYWIT: Pray, do not handle me, sir.

SPUNKY: Faith, y'are too nice, lady. And, as for my secrecy, you know I have vowed it often to you.

FOLLYWIT: You have? But of course. But no, no, you men are fickle –

SPUNKY: Fickle? God's foot, pull my chain, lady –

FOLLYWIT: I shall pull your chain. *(Takes SPUNKY's chain.)* And return it tomorrow. Meet me in the snug at The Suck And Swallow tavern 'tween nine and ten.

SPUNKY: And if I do not, lady, let me lose it, thy love and my best fortunes.

FOLLYWIT: Speak no more; go to.

SPUNKY: Farewell, sweet Lady.

SPUNKY kisses him/her and exits.

FOLLYWIT: By my faith, I perceive by his action toward my middle region there has been some saucy nibbling motion 'tween Master Spunky and the cunning nestlecock. I'll teach the slave to be so bold yet, as once to offer to vault into his master's saddle. Now, casket, by your leave, I have seen your outside oft, but thats no proof. Some have fair outsides that are nothing worth. *(Opens casket.)* Ha, diamond, ruby, sapphire! This is the fruit of old grunting venery. Uncle you may thank your cockatrice for this; to keep a whore to hinder your nephew, 'tis 'gainst nature i'faith!

Enter SIR BOUNTEOUS.

SIR BOUNTEOUS: Ah! Methink I feel myself well toasted, bumbasted, rubbed and refreshed.

He grabs FOLLYWIT and kisses him/her.

SIR BOUNTEOUS: *(Aside.)* But i'faith I cannot forget to think how soon sickness has altered her. By the mass, methinks her breath has much ado to be sweet. Like a thing compounded of wine, beer and tobacco. And I smell much pudding on't. I'll kiss the lower end.

FOLLYWIT: Ay, perhaps that's the sweeter!

SIR BOUNTEOUS: I think I have bestirred my stumps, i'faith. O dash my doodle! I was pumped up before, I am punctured now. Spunky, I have need of my tincture! The bald-headed hermit is returning to his cave! Be patient, lady. My tincture, Spunky!

SIR BOUNTEOUS exits. FOLLYWIT grabs some valuables.

FOLLYWIT: Who keeps a harlot tell him this from me,
He needs nor thief, disease, nor enemy.

FOLLYWIT exits. SIR BOUNTEOUS returns.

SIR BOUNTEOUS: How does thou now, sweet girl…? Speak, ha? Wench? Why body of me, what's here? My casket, broke open, my jewels stolen. Spunky!

SPUNKY: *(Off.)* Sir?

SIR BOUNTEOUS: Come hither, Spunky!

SPUNKY: *(Off.)* I'll find a time anon, sir. Your worship's still at the four-legged frolic.

SIR BOUNTEOUS: Why, Spunky!

SPUNKY: Very well, though you'll make me blush i'faith, sir. *(Enters.)*

SIR BOUNTEOUS: Where's this creature?

SPUNKY: What creature is't you'd have, sir?

SIR BOUNTEOUS: The worst that ever breathes.

SPUNKY: That's a wild boar, sir.

SIR BOUNTEOUS: That's a vile whore, sir. Where went she, rascal?

SPUNKY: Who? Your recreation, sir.

SIR BOUNTEOUS: No, my execration, sir! A pox engross her! See you this casket, sir.

SPUNKY: My chain, my chain, my chain, my one and only chain!

Exits.

SIR BOUNTEOUS: Is not whoring enough to answer for, but she must join thievery to't. Burgling buttock-broker! Nay I ha' done with her i'faith.
Did she want anything? Was she not supplied?
Nay and liberally, for that's an old man's sin.
We'll feast our lechery though we starve our kin.
Is not my name Sir Bounteous? Am I not expressed there?
Ah fie, fie, fie, fie, fie, but I perceive
Though she have never so complete a friend

A strumpet's love will have a stinky end: Truly Kidman!
I can hardly bear this. But say I should complain. God's
foot, the judges will but laugh at it and bid her borrow
more money of 'em. I saw the same case tried at Newbury.
Well, things must slip and sleep;
I will dissemble it, and be Bounteous still.
The masque I wear shall be a good for all,
A party! A masque! I'll host a ball!
(Exits.) Spunky! Rinse your gums with mull-sack!

4.4

The LITTLEDICKS' house. BROTHEL knocks on the door.

MRS LITTLEDICK: Who's that knocks?

BROTHEL: A friend. *(Enters.)*

MRS LITTLEDICK: Why, how now, sir? This was desperately
adventured. I thought not to see you until the morrow.

BROTHEL: No? Why what made you at my chamber then
even now?

MRS LITTLEDICK: I, at your chamber?

BROTHEL: Puh, dissemble not, come, come, you were there.

MRS LITTLEDICK: By my life, you wrong me, sir.

BROTHEL: What?

MRS LITTLEDICK: First, y'are not ignorant what watch keeps
o're me;
And for your chamber, as I live, I know't not.

BROTHEL: Burst into sorrow then, and grief's extremes,
Whilst I beat on this flesh.

MRS LITTLEDICK: What is't disturbs you, sir?

BROTHEL: Then was the devil in your likeness there.

MRS LITTLEDICK: Ha?

BROTHEL: A she-devil did assume thee formally,
    That face, that voice, that gesture, that attire,
    E'en as it sits on thee, not a pleat altered,
    That skirt so snug about the hips, those raven stockings,
    As if the fashion were her own invention –

MRS LITTLEDICK: Mercy defend me!

BROTHEL: To beguile me more. The cunning succubus
    Wept to me, laid my vows before me, urged me,
    Gave me the private marks of all our love,
    Wooed me in wanton and effeminate rhymes,
    And sung and danced about me like a fairy;
    And had not worthier cogitations blessed me
    Thy form and her enchantments would have possessed me.

MRS LITTLEDICK: What shall become of me? My own feelings
    doom me.

BROTHEL: Forgive me Mistress Littledick, on my soul
    The guilt hangs double:
    My lust and my enticement of you.
    What knows the lecher when he tups his whore
    Whether it be the devil his parts adore?
    They're both so like, that in our natural sense
    I could discern no change nor difference.
    No marvel then that times should stretch and turn;
    None care for religion, all for pleasure burn.
    Holy zeal into hot lust is now transformed,
    Faith into fancy hair, hope into powdered faces,
    Charity into wanton nethergarments.
    Why, even The Good Samaritan now keeps a bumworker!

*He runs from MRS LITTLEDICK and kneels remorsefully.
MR LITTLEDICK enters unnoticed.*

BROTHEL: Live honest, and live happy, keep thy vows;
    She's part a virgin whom but one man knows.
    Embrace thy husband, and beside him none;

Having but one heart, give it but to one.

MRS LITTLEDICK: I vow it on my knees, with tears true bred,
No man shall ever wrong my husband's bed.

BROTHEL: Rise, I'm thy friend forever.

MR LITTLEDICK: And I thine forever and ever.
Let me embrace thee, sir, whom I will love,
Even next unto my soul.
Two dear rare gems this hour presents me with,
A wife that's modest and a friend that's right.
Idle suspicion and fear, now take your flight.

BROTHEL: A happy inward peace crown both your joys.

MR LITTLEDICK: Thanks above utterance to you.

MR LITTLEDICK's phone rings.

MR LITTLEDICK: Now, the news?

SPUNKY: *(On the other end.)* Sir Bounteous Peersucker, sir,
invites you and your honoured wife to a feast and revels on
Tuesday next. Jacobean garb.

MR LITTLEDICK: Reply with both our willingness and thanks.
(Hangs up.) I will entreat you, friend, to be my guest.

BROTHEL: Who, I sir?

MR LITTLEDICK: Faith, you shall.

BROTHEL: *(Aside.)* Oh, trouble and strife.

MR LITTLEDICK: You'll sit with me and stimulate my wife.

MRS LITTLEDICK sings 'Cry Me A River'.

4.6

Outside The Moka Bar. FOLLYWIT is coming on to TRULY KIDMAN.

FOLLYWIT: Why, here's a woman made as a man would wish
to have her.
What so coy, so strict? Come, come.

TRULY KIDMAN: *(Talking posh.)* Pray, change your opinion, sir; I am not for that use.

FOLLYWIT: Will you but hear me?

TRULY KIDMAN: No, for fear I shall hear that which I would not.

TRULY KIDMAN leaves and FOLLYWIT is bereft.

FOLLYWIT: 'Tis the maddest, fantastical'st girl: I never knew so much flesh and so much nimbleness put together.
I do protest in earnest, I ne'er saw
Face worth my object 'til mine eyes met hers.

Enter MRS KIDMAN.

FOLLYWIT: By your favour, lady.

MRS KIDMAN: You're welcome, sir.

FOLLYWIT: Know you the young gentlewoman that went by lately?

MRS KIDMAN: I have best cause to know her; I'm her mother, sir.

FOLLYWIT: Oh, in good time. I like the gentlewoman well; a pretty-contrived beauty.

MRS KIDMAN: Ay, nature has done her part, sir.

FOLLYWIT: But she has one uncomely quality.

MRS KIDMAN: What's that, sir?

FOLLYWIT: God's foot, she's afraid of a man.

MRS KIDMAN: Alas, 'tis her bashful spirit; she's fearful of her honour.

FOLLYWIT: Of her honour? God's eyelid, I'm sure I cannot get her maidenhead with breathing upon her, nor can she lose her honour in her tongue.

MRS KIDMAN: True, and I have often told her so, but this is the way of a foolish virgin, sir. Always timorsome, always backward. Ah, that same peevish honour of hers has undone her and me both, good gentleman. The suitors, the jewels, the alliances that have been offered her! We could have been made women for ever. But what was her fashion? She could not endure the sight of a man forsooth, would run to her chamber, open her good book and lose herself in its well-thumbed passages.

FOLLYWIT: Have you not so much power with her to command her presence?

MRS KIDMAN: You shall see straight what I can do, sir.

Exits.

FOLLYWIT: Would I might be hanged, if my love do not stretch to her deeper and deeper; those bashful maiden humours take me prisoner.

WAITRESS: Yeah.

FOLLYWIT: When there comes a restraint on't upon flesh, we are always most greedy upon't, and that's what makes your merchant's wife oftentimes pay so dear for a mouthful. Give me a woman as she was made at first: simple of herself, without sophistication, like this pure virgin. I cannot abide them when they have tricks, set speeches and artful entertainments. If e'er I love, or anything move me, 'twill be a woman's simple modesty.

Enter MRS KIDMAN. She brings her daughter who plays at being reluctant, bashful and virginal.

TRULY KIDMAN: Pray, let me go! Why, mother what do you mean? I beseech you, mother? Is this your conquest now? Great glory 'tis to o'ercome a poor and silly virgin.

FOLLYWIT: The wonder of our time sits in that brow,
I ne'er beheld a perfect maid 'til now.

MRS KIDMAN: Thou childish thing, more bashful then thou'rt wise.
Why dost thou turn aside and drown thine eyes?
Look, fearful fool, there's no temptation near thee;

Art not ashamed that any flesh should fear thee?
Why, I durst pawn my life the gentleman means no other
But honest and pure love to thee; how say you, sir?

FOLLYWIT: By my faith, not I, lady.

MRS KIDMAN: Hark you there? What grieves your honour
now?
What lascivious breath intends to rear
Against that maiden organ your chaste ear?
Repent you now of your opinion past;
Men love as purely as you can be chaste.
To her yourself, sir, the way's broke before you,
You have the easier passage.

FOLLYWIT: Fear not, come; erect thy sweetness in thy look.
I am no curious wooer, but, i'faith,
I love thee honourably.

TRULY KIDMAN: How mean you that, sir?

FOLLYWIT: God's foot, as one loves a woman for a wife.

MRS KIDMAN: Has the gentleman answered you?

FOLLYWIT: I do confess it truely to you both,
My estate is yet but sickly, but I've an uncle, Sir Bounteous
Peersucker, will make me lord of thousands at his death.

MRS KIDMAN: I know your uncle well; she knows him better.

FOLLYWIT: Why then, you know no fiction. My estate is
prodigious, my endowment beyond measure.

MRS KIDMAN: Nay, daughter, he says true.

FOLLYWIT: And thou shalt often ride upon't, and come to
know its every inch.

MRS KIDMAN: Ah, 'twill be a merry journey.

FOLLYWIT: What, is't a match? Shall I make bold with your
finger, gentlewoman? If't be clap hands and lips!

MRS KIDMAN: 'Tis done, there's witness on't.

WAITRESS: Yeah.

FOLLYWIT: Why then, mother, I salute you.

MRS KIDMAN: Son Follywit, come hither. If I might counsel
thee, we'll e'en take her while the good mood's upon her.

FOLLYWIT: By my troth, agreed, mother.

MRS KIDMAN: *(Aside to TRULY KIDMAN.)* Send for a priest.

Exit TRULY KIDMAN.

MRS KIDMAN: *(To FOLLYWIT.)* Nor does her wealth consist all
in her flesh,

Though beauty be enough wealth for a woman.

She brings a dowry of three hundred pound with her.

FOLLYWIT: God's foot, that will serve 'til my uncle die.

MRS KIDMAN: Is he not a lusty old gentleman, sir? I did hear
he still rides with Viscount Hunt.

FOLLYWIT: Troth, he's given to women; he keeps a strumpet
presently.

MRS KIDMAN: Fie.

FOLLYWIT: Do not tell my wife on't.

MRS KIDMAN: That were needless, i'faith.

TRULY KIDMAN returns.

TRULY KIDMAN: *(Aside to MRS KIDMAN.)* We'll be clapped up
within the hour.

FOLLYWIT: Wife, my uncle makes a great fancy dress ball
upon the 'leventh of this month, tuesday next. And I have
a mind that you shall see some actors there. I have one
trick more to put upon him. My wife and yourself shall go
thither before as my guests, and prove his entertainment.
I'll meet you there at night. That feast which he makes will,
unknown to him, serve fitly for our wedding dinner. And
the jest will be here, to hear of this match will finish him
off!

TRULY AND MRS KIDMAN: Yes!

MRS KIDMAN: An excellent course, i'faith, and a thrifty. Why, son, methinks you begin to thrive before y'are married.

FOLLYWIT: We shall thrive one day, love, and money enough. Between our hopes there's but an old man's puff.

FOLLYWIT sings.

SONG: *'YOU UPSET ME, BABY'* by Riley B King and Jules Bihari

Exit FOLLYWIT. The KIDMANS drop their act and become common again.

MRS KIDMAN: So, girl, here was a bird well caught.

TRULY KIDMAN: If ever! But what of Sir Bounteous. 'Twill scarce please him well.

MRS KIDMAN: Who covets fruit, ne'er cares from whence it fell,

Thou'st wedded youth and strength, and wealth will fall. Last thou'rt made honest.

TRULY KIDMAN: And thats worth 'em all.

5.1

SIR BOUNTEOUS' great hall. SIR BOUNTEOUS is finishing getting dressed in Jacobean garb.

SIR BOUNTEOUS: Have a care, Spunky! Cast an eye into'th'kitchen; o'erlook the knaves a little. Every Jack has his friend today. This cousin and that cousin drops by for a dish of meat; a man knows not 'til he make a feast how many varlets he feeds. God's foot, I swear they smell my kitchen seven mile about.

Enter the LITTLEDICKS with BROTHEL. Like all the guests that follow, they are dressed in Jacobean garb for the fancy dress party.

MR LITTLEDICK: Good Sir Bounteous.

SIR BOUNTEOUS: Ah, Mister Littledick and his sweet
    bedfellow! Y'are very copiously welcome. Here, eat some
    plums!

MR LITTLEDICK: Sir, here's an especial dear friend of ours; we
    were bold to make his way to your table.

SIR BOUNTEOUS: Thanks for that boldnesse e'er, good Master
    Littledick. Is this your friend, sir?

MR LITTLEDICK: Both my wife's friend and mine, sir.

SIR. BOUNTEOUS: Why then compendiously, sir, y'are
    omnivorously welcome.

BROTHEL: I thank you, sir.

SIR BOUNTEOUS: Ha, excellently retorted i'faith! What a wit!
    Walk in, sweet gentlemen, walk in. There's a good fire it'h
    hall. You shall have my sweet company instantly.

MR LITTLEDICK: Ay, good Sir Bounteous.

Enter SPUNKY.

SIR BOUNTEOUS: How now, what news brings thee in
    stumbling now?

SPUNKY: There are certain actor-types come to town, sir, and
    desire to present themselves before your worship.

SIR BOUNTEOUS: Actors-types? By the mass, they are
    welcome! They'll grace my entertainment well, but are
    they good?

SPUNKY: I know not, i'faith.

SIR BOUNTEOUS: For some know not when to play, where
    to play, nor what to play; not when to play for fearful
    fools, where to play for prudish fools, nor what to play for
    critical fools. Go, call 'em in. *(Exit SPUNKY.)* How fitly the
    whoresons come upo'th'feast; troth, this evening was in
    want of proper actors. Oh, welcome, welcome my friends!

Enter FOLLYWIT and his men as actors.

FOLLYWIT: The month of May delights not in her flowers,

More then we joy in that sweet sight of yours.

SIR BOUNTEOUS: Bravo! Well acted o' my credit, I perceive he's your best actor.

SPONGER: He is most convincing, sir.

SIR BOUNTEOUS: What, what? Put on your hat, sir. Pray, put on! And whose men are you I pray? Nay, keep on your hat still.

FOLLYWIT: We serve my Lord Owemuch, sir.

SIR BOUNTEOUS: My Lord Owemuch? By my troth, the welcomest men alive! Give me all your hands at once. That honourable gentleman? He lay at my house in a robbery once, and took all quietly, went away cheerfully. I never saw a man of honour bear things bravelier away. Good egg! Serve my Lord Owemuch? Welcome, i'faith. Some bastard for my lord's players; where be your boys who play girls?

FOLLYWIT: Bringing up the rear, sir.

SIR BOUNTEOUS: Good, good, and which is the manager amongst you; which is he? Come, be not afraid.

FOLLYWIT: I am he, sir.

SIR BOUNTEOUS: Art thou he? Give me thy hand. Harke in thine ear; thou rollest too fast to gather so much moss as thy fellows there; champ upon that. Ha, and what play shall we have my masters?

FOLLYWIT: A witty, if earthy Comedy sir. And yet one which lays bare the intertwined pursuits of passion, money, power and religion. 'T'as been well-receiv'd in the provinces, sir.

SIR BOUNTEOUS: I and my guests may laugh a little. What's the name on't?

FOLLYWIT: 'Tis called *The Slip*. We'll be giving you *The Slip*.

SIR BOUNTEOUS: *The Slip*? By my troth, a pretty name, and a glib one. Go all and slip into't as fast as you can, ha!

Exuent FOLLYWIT and friends.

Enter MASTER WHOPPING-PROSPECT and MASTER MUCHLY-MINTED.

SIR BOUNTEOUS: Welcome, gentlemen, welcome. Why, this will be a true feast, a top-class supper, we're going to have a play and everything!

MASTER WHOPPING-PROSPECT: Ooh, prick that down!

They go within.

SIR BOUNTEOUS: More lights!

Enter THE KIDMANS.

SIR BOUNTEOUS: I called for light and here come a light-fingered pair. A choice of stinks indeed! Dare the thief look me i'th face? O impudent times! But I shan't let on.

MRS KIDMAN: Bless you, Sir Bounteous.

SIR BOUNTEOUS: O welcome, welcome… Thief, whore, pimp! Welcome all three.

MRS KIDMAN: Nay, here's but two on's, sir.

SIR BOUNTEOUS: O, m'troth, I took her for a couple. I'd have sworn there had been two faces there.

MRS KIDMAN: I'll make it hold, sir, my daughter is a couple: she was married yesterday.

SIR BOUNTEOUS: Buz, he cannot be but a rascal. Walk in, walk in, bold guests that come unsent for. *Ferter ut opibus abundud maximis!*

MRS KIDMAN: *Ferter and abundundis?* He calls me an old fart!

SIR BOUNTEOUS: *(Stops TRULY KIDMAN.)* Soft Truly Kidman, I perceive where my jewels went now: to grace your marriage.

TRULY KIDMAN: Sir?

SIR BOUNTEOUS: Ay; how happ't it wench? You put the slip upon me

Not three nights since. You will not deny this, I trust?

TRULY KIDMAN: I will, and with a safe conscience, sir.

The KIDMANS go within.

SIR BOUNTEOUS: O audacious age!
    She denies me and all, when on her fingers,
    I spied the ruby sit that does betray her,
    And blushes for her fact.
    Oh, quim-whiskers:
    Feast, mirth, ay, harmony, and the play to boot!
    A jovial season. How now, are you ready?

Enter FOLLYWIT, SPONGER and OBOE with their booty.

FOLLYWIT: Even upon readiness, sir. We have borrowed some of your property for properties.

SIR BOUNTEOUS: Keep you your hat on.

FOLLYWIT: Sir, to convince in our comedy we would be bold to require your worship's assistance.

SIR BOUNTEOUS: Why, with all my heart, what is't you want? Speak!

FOLLYWIT: One's a gold chain for a justice's hat, sir.

SIR BOUNTEOUS: Why here, here whoreson, will this serve your turn?

FOLLYWIT: Excellent well, sir.

SIR BOUNTEOUS: What else lack you?

FOLLYWIT: We should use a ring with a stone in't.

SIR BOUNTEOUS: Nay, whoops, I have given too many rings already. Talk no more of rings I pray you, here, here, here, make this jewel serve for once.

FOLLYWIT: Oh, this will serve, sir.

SIR BOUNTEOUS: What, have you all now?

FOLLYWIT: All now, sir. Only time is of great consequence i'th middle of the play, and I would desire your worship's watch.

SIR BOUNTEOUS: My watch, with all my heart, only request the actor be not fiddling with it. 'Tis a delicate new Swiss creation that doth chime upon the hour.

FOLLYWIT: And now we are furnished, I shall acquit Sir Bounteous to entertain his guests.

SPONGER and OBOE scarper…

SIR BOUNTEOUS: But now you are furnished, sir, you must entertain us. The play must begin. Come, more lights, more stools! Sir Aquitaine and Sir Skunknodger. The play begins!

The guests gather, boxing FOLLYWIT in.

MR LITTLEDICK: Have you players here, Sir Bounteous?

SIR BOUNTEOUS: We have 'em for you, sir. Fine, nimble comedians; proper actors most of them.

BROTHEL: Whose men, I pray you, sir?

SIR BOUNTEOUS: Oh, there's their credit, sir. They serve an honourable, popular gentleman, yclipped my Lord Owemuch. He was in Ireland lately. And Spain. And very much in the island of Cyprus, I'm told.

MR LITTLEDICK: How is the comedy called, Sir Bounteous?

SIR BOUNTEOUS: Marry, sir, *The Slip*.

MR LITTLEDICK: *The Slip*?

SIR BOUNTEOUS: Ay, and here the prologue begins to slip in upon's!

FOLLYWIT embarks upon an improvised prologue…

FOLLYWIT: We sing of wand'ring knights, what them betide,
Who nor in one place, nor one shape abide.
They're in this room but no police can reach 'em,

Like vapours i'th'air you'll not impeach 'em.
The play which we present, no fault shall meet
But one, you'll say 'tis short, we'll say 'tis sweet.
'Tis given much to dumb shows, which some praise,
And lengthy costume changes – expect delays!
So, to conclude, and give the name her due:
The play is calld *The Slip*, I vanish too.

Exit.

SIR BOUNTEOUS: Excellently well acted, and a nimble conceit.

MR LITTLEDICK: The Prologue's pretty i'faith.

BROTHEL: And went off well.

TRULY KIDMAN: O'my troth, if I were not married, I could find in my heart to fall in love with that player now; truly I find his part delights me. Mine own parts have been played many times and often; with desire counterfeit my heart was my own, yet now made honest my own heart is blown. I would bid him to a supper – many's the actor has feasted in my private rooms – but I desire and count him fit, to play me truly and eat my banquet.

Pause as they wait for the players' return.

SIR BOUNTEOUS: But, passion of me, where be these knaves? Methinks they stay very long.

BROTHEL: Oh you must bear a little, sir. They have many costume changes.

SIR BOUNTEOUS: Costume change? Troth, 'tis a horrible long thing.

FOLLYWIT runs back in, looking for a way out.

FOLLYWIT: A pox of such fortune! The plot's betrayed! I shall be shamed forever!

MR LITTLEDICK: How moodily he walks; what plays he? An angry young man? I ha' seen such a man at The Royal Court!

SIR BOUNTEOUS: He's an unfortunate justice, upon my credit. I know by the chain there.

FOLLYWIT: *(Aside.)* Invention stick to me this once. 'Unfortunate justice!'

SIR BOUNTEOUS: Said I so!

FOLLYWIT: 'In my kin unfortunate,
Brought by a constable before me, my kin associate with him.
Twice have I set him free from officers' fangs.
My conscience will permit but once more.
For should the Law seize him,
Being kin to me, 'twould blemish much my name!'

SIR BOUNTEOUS: Cuds, how true! Should the law seize kin'o'mine, I'd do th'same.

Enter CONSTABLE with OBOE and SPONGER. They have been arrested.

CONSTABLE: That's it, hop to, raggedy rascals! To sit before the victim of thy felony!

SPONGER: God's foot, 'tis Follywit.

OBOE: I had thought he 'scaped.

FOLLYWIT: 'How now, Constable, what news with thee?'

CONSTABLE: May it please your worship sir, here are a company of naughty fellows.

SIR BOUNTEOUS: He speaks to me? My, this work is experimental! Turn to th'justice, you lobcock.

FOLLYWIT: 'What's the matter, Constable, whats the matter?'

CONSTABLE: I have nothing to say to you. They were making off, sir, an't please your worship.

SIR BOUNTEOUS: Yet again he speaks to me. Talk to thy fellow players, bufflehead!

FOLLYWIT: 'Why, sure the Constable speaks to the wall, he's drunk.'

SPONGER: *(Catching on.)* 'We spied that weakness in him long ago, sir. Only in respect of his office we obeyed him, for I protest, sir, he found us but walking along.'

FOLLYWIT: 'Constable, this is outrageous!'

CONSTABLE: I'faith, speak not to me, scoundrel!

FOLLYWIT: 'Are your wits steeped? I'll make you an example for all dizzy constables!'

SIR BOUNTEOUS: Well said, Justice; he helps his kinsmen well.

FOLLYWIT: 'How they abuse justice. Here, bind him to this chair.'

CONSTABLE: Ha, bind me?

FOLLYWIT: We want cord.

TRULY KIDMAN: Use garters!

All the women throw their garters. The CONSTABLE is bound to a chair with them.

CONSTABLE: Help, help, gentlemen!

SPONGER: I am helping!

CONSTABLE: They're thieves, thieves!

FOLLYWIT: 'A gag will help all this. Keep less noise, you knave!'

CONSTABLE: Oh, help, rescue me!

SIR BOUNTEOUS: Ho, ho, ho, ho!

FOLLYWIT: 'Constable, we leave to find physic for your ailing brain. Anon.'

CONSTABLE: *(Through gag.)* They are robbers! They're robbers!

FOLLYWIT and his friends depart to much laughter.

SIR BOUNTEOUS: Ha, ha, ha! By my troth, the maddest piece of justice, gentlemen, that ever was committed.

MR LITTLEDICK: I'll be sworn for the madness on't, sir.

SIR BOUNTEOUS: I am deceived if this prove not a merry comedy and a witty one.

CONSTABLE: They are robbers!

BROTHEL: Alas, poor constable, his mouth's open and ne'er a wise word.

CONSTABLE: *(Muffled.)* They're getting away!

SIR BOUNTEOUS: He turns and tells his tale to me like an ass. What have I to do with their getting away?

MRS LITTLEDICK: But what follows all this while, sir? Methinks some character should pass by before this time and pity the constable.

SIR BOUNTEOUS: By'th'mass, and you say true, sir. Go, sirrah, step in; I think they have lost their own plot, forgot their themselves. Call the knaves back.

A SERVANT goes to bring the actors back.

CONSTABLE: *(Muffled.)* Call them back, call them back!

SIR BOUNTEOUS: Hark, the constable agrees! He says call 'em back!

SERVANT returns.

SIR BOUNTEOUS: How now? When come they?

SERVANT: Alas, an't please your worship, there's not one of them to be found, sir.

SIR BOUNTEOUS: How?

MASTER MUCHLY-MINTED: What says the fellow?

SIR BOUNTEOUS: Body of me, thou liest!

SERVANT: Not a hair, sir.

MR LITTLEDICK: How now, Sir Bounteous?

SIR BOUNTEOUS: Cheated and defeated! Ungag that rascal, I'll make him bring 'em out. Cuds, I want to know what happens next!

CONSTABLE: Did not I tell your worship this before? I brought 'em before you for suspected persons, made signs that my very jaw bone aches! Your worship would not hear me, called me ass, laughed at me!

SIR BOUNTEOUS: Ha?

MASTER WHOPPING-PROSPECT: Ah! I begin to taste it.

SIR BOUNTEOUS: Give me leave, why art not thou the constable i'th'comedy?

CONSTABLE: I'th'comedy? No, I am the constable in a very tragedy, sir.

SIR BOUNTEOUS: I am fooled, i'faith, I am fooled! I was never so disgraced since the hour my mother whipped me!

BROTHEL: I seldom heard jest match it.

MRS LITTLEDICK: Nor I, i'faith.

SIR BOUNTEOUS: Gentlemen, shall I entreat a courtesy?

MR LITTLEDICK: What is't, sir?

SIR BOUNTEOUS: Do not laugh at me seven year hence.

BROTHEL: We should betray and laugh at our own folly then, for by my troth all here were deceived

SIR BOUNTEOUS: Faith, that's some comfort yet. Ha, ha, it was deftly carried. Troth, I commend their wits. Before our faces they make us asses while we sit there laughing at ourselves.

BROTHEL: Faith, they were guileful swindlers.

SIR BOUNTEOUS: Why, they confessed so much themselves. They said they'd give us the slip; they should be men of their words. Though I hope the fellow that played the justice will have more conscience i'faith, than to carry away a chain worth a hundred marks. But methinks my

Lord Owemuch's players should not scorn me so i'faith; they will come and bring all again, I know.

CONSTABLE: They're not really actors! You've been duped.

CONSTABLE moves to exit as FOLLYWIT and cohorts enter as party guests in Jacobean fancy dress.

CONSTABLE: Evening, sir.

Exits.

FOLLYWIT: Pray, uncle, give me your blessing?

SIR BOUNTEOUS: Who? Nephew Follywit? I haven't seen this man for five years, though to see him standing before me now, methinks he's never been away. Rise richer by a blessing; thou art welcome!

FOLLYWIT: Thanks, good uncle. I was bold to bring these gentlemen, my friends.

SIR BOUNTEOUS: They're all welcome.

FOLLYWIT: *(Aside to TRULY KIDMAN.)* Our marriage known?

TRULY KIDMAN: *(Aside to FOLLYWIT.)* Not a word yet.

FOLLYWIT: The better.

SIR BOUNTEOUS: Faith, son, would you had come sooner with these gentlemen.

FOLLYWIT: Why, uncle?

SIR BOUNTEOUS: We had a play here.

FOLLYWIT: A play, sir? No.

SIR BOUNTEOUS: Yes, faith, a pox o'th'author. And the actors were terrible!

FOLLYWIT: Bless us all! Why, were they such vile ones, sir?

SIR BOUNTEOUS: I am sure villanous ones, sir.

FOLLYWIT: What, sir?

SIR BOUNTEOUS: Which way came you, gentlemen? You could not choose but meet 'em.

FOLLYWIT: We met a company with hampers after 'em.

SIR BOUNTEOUS: Oh, those were they, those were they. They have hampered me finely, sirrah.

FOLLYWIT: How, sir?

SIR BOUNTEOUS: How, sir? I lent the rascals properties to furnish out their play, a chain, a jewel, and a watch, and they watched their time made away with 'em.

FOLLYWIT: Such villainous creatures!

A watch chimes.

SIR BOUNTEOUS: Hark, hark, gentlemen! By this light, the watch rings in a pocket! Whose is't, whose ist? By'th'mass, 'tis he; hast thou my watch, son? I now look for mine again, i'faith.

SIR BOUNTEOUS goes for FOLLYWIT's pockets but FOLLYWIT resists.

SIR BOUNTEOUS: I spy a telling bulge if not mistook. Nay, let me feel for't. Ah! I have my hands upon the prize!

FOLLYWIT: Argh!

MASTER WHOPPING-PROSPECT: Great or small?

SIR BOUNTEOUS: At once I have drawn chain, jewel, watch and all!

BROTHEL: By my faith, you have a fortunate hand, sir.

MR LITTLEDICK: Nay, all to come at once.

SPONGER: A vengeance of our foolery.

FOLLYWIT: Have I 'scaped the constable to be brought in by the watch?

TRULY KIDMAN: Oh destiny! Have I married a thief, mother?

MRS KIDMAN: Comfort thyself; thou fooled him first. He believed you a virgin.

LITTLEDICK: What?

SIR BOUNTEOUS: Why, son, how long have you been my Lord Owemuch's servants, i'faith?

FOLLYWIT: Faith, uncle, shall I be true to you?

SIR BOUNTEOUS: I think 'tis time.

FOLLYWIT: I, knowing the day of your feast, and the natural inclination you have to pleasure and pastime, presumed upon your patience for a jest.

SIR BOUNTEOUS: Sir?

FOLLYWIT: And that you may be seriously assured of my herafter stableness of life, I have took another course.

SIR BOUNTEOUS: What?

FOLLYWIT: Took a wife.

SIR BOUNTEOUS: A wife? God's foot, what fool would marry thee, a madman? When was the wedding kept in Bedlam?

FOLLYWIT: She's both a gentlewoman and a virgin.

SIR BOUNTEOUS: Stop there, stop there; would I might see her?

FOLLYWIT: You have your wish; she's here.

He gestures to TRULY KIDMAN.

MASTER MUCHLY-MINTED
AND MASTER WHOPPING-PROSPECT: Dash it!

SIR BOUNTEOUS: Ah, ha, ha, ha! This makes amends for all.

FOLLYWIT: How now?

SPONGER: Captain, do you hear? Is she your wife in earnest?

FOLLYWIT: How then?

SPONGER: Nothing but pity you, sir.

SIR BOUNTEOUS: Speak, son, is't true? Can you fool us and let a fly-girl, a pole-climber, a fuckstress fool you? That woman is my mistress.

FOLLYWIT: Ha!

TRULY KIDMAN: What I have been is past; be that forgiven,
And have a soul true both to thee and heaven.

FOLLYWIT: Craft recoils in the end like an over-charged musket,
And maims the very hand that puts fire to it.
Does not he return wisest, that comes whipped with his own follies? All toast!

ALL: Hear, hear.

SIR BOUNTEOUS: The best is, sirrah, you toast none but me;
And since I drink the top, take her; and hark,
I spice the bottom with a thousand mark.

He gives FOLLYWIT a wad of cash and slaps TRULY KIDMAN on the bum.

FOLLYWIT: What base birth does not raiment make glorious?

TRULY KIDMAN: And this raiment, when removed, will give you glory, husband.

FOLLYWIT and TRULY KIDMAN kiss.

FOLLYWIT: By my troth, she is as good a cup of nectar as any bachelor needs to sip at.

SIR BOUNTEOUS: Come, gentlemen, to'th'feast, let not time waste;
We have pleased our ear, now let us please our taste.
Who lives by cunning, mark it, his fate's cast;
When he has fooled all, then is himself fooled last.

SONG: *'WHO WILL THE NEXT FOOL BE'*
by Charlie Rich

The End.

SONG: *'IF I CAN'T SELL IT, I'LL KEEP SITTIN' ON IT'*
by Alexander Hill and Andy Razaf

WWW.OBERONBOOKS.COM

 Follow us on www.twitter.com/@oberonbooks
& www.facebook.com/oberonbook